AQA Introduction

Nelson Thornes has worked in partnership with AQA to ensure this book and the accompanying online resources offer you the best support for your A Level course.

All resources have been approved by senior AQA examiners so you can feel assured that they closely match the specification for this subject and provide you with everything you need to prepare successfully for your exams.

These print and online resources together **unlock blended learning**; this means that the links between the activities in the book and the activities online blend together to maximise your understanding of a topic and help you achieve your potential.

These online resources are available on **kerboodle!** which can be accessed via the internet at **www.kerboodle.com/live**, anytime, anywhere. If your school or college subscribes to this service you will be provided with your own personal login details. Once logged in, access your course and locate the required activity.

For more information and help visit **www.kerboodle.com**

Icons in this book indicate where there is material online related to that topic. The following icons are used:

Learning activity

These resources include a variety of interactive and non-interactive activities to support your learning:

- Animations
- Presentations
- Simple interactive activities
- Worksheet activities
- Glossary.

Progress tracking

These resources include a variety of tests that you can use to check your knowledge on particular topics (Test yourself) and a range of resources that enable you to analyse and understand examination questions (On your marks…).

Research support

These resources include WebQuests, in which you are assigned a task and provided with a range of weblinks to use as source material for research. These are designed as extension resources to stretch you and broaden your learning, in order for you to attain the highest possible marks in your exams.

Coursework activity

This icon indicates where there are resources that will assist you as your work through your project.

Study skills

These resources are designed to help students develop skills that are key to this course, for example, in identifying ICT problems and solutions and for their coursework. These resources include, text and image analysis tools, discussion tools, a study kit to guide your coursework and video and audio interviews.

Practical activity

This icon signals where there is a relevant practical activity to be undertaken on a computer. Where indicated, support is provided online.

Weblinks

Our online resources feature a list of recommended weblinks, split by chapter. This will give you a head start, helping you to navigate to the best websites that will aid your learning and understanding of the topics in your course.

How to use this book

This book covers the specification for your course and is arranged in a sequence approved by AQA. The main text of the book will cover Units 3 and 4 of the AQA A Level ICT specification. These units account for 30 per cent and 20 per cent, respectively, of the overall A Level mark.

Unit 3 examines the rapidly changing world of ICT, considering technological change and the development of systems within organisations. It considers the importance of good quality information to large organisations and how the ICT systems are used to provide it. Within this unit you will also build on the knowledge and skills necessary to complete your A Level coursework.

Unit 4 offers step-by-step guidance for creating your coursework project. By working through this unit, and in completing each of the activities, you will build a comprehensive ICT project that addresses each of the criteria on AQA's marking grid.

Unit openers give you a summary of the content you will be covering and give a brief context for each topic/section.

The features in this book include:

Learning objectives

At the beginning of each section you will find a list of learning objectives that contain targets linked to the requirements of the specification. The relevant specification reference is also provided.

Key terms

Terms that you will need to be able to define and understand are highlighted in bold blue type within the text, e.g. **just in time**. You can look up these terms in the glossary.

Case studies

Real-life examples to illustrate a point.

Did you know?

Interesting facts to bring learning to life.

Remember

Key points and common errors.

Activities

Suggestions for practical activities you can carry out.

PC activities

PC-based activities that will support you in developing skills which are key to the course.

Coursework activities

These offer guidance as you work through your A2 project.

End of sub-topic questions

Short questions that test your understanding of the subject and allow you to apply the knowledge and skills you have acquired to different scenarios.

AQA Examiner's tip

Hints from AQA examiners to help you with your studies and to prepare you for your exam.

AQA Examination-style questions

Questions in the style that you can expect in your exam. These occur at the end of each unit to give practice in examination-style questions for a particular topic.

AQA examination questions are reproduced by permission of the Assessment and Qualifications Alliance.

Nelson Thornes is responsible for the solution(s) given and they may not constitute the only possible solution(s).

Web links for this book

All websites that you will need to access when using this book can be found at: www.nelsonthornes.com/aqagce/ict_book_links.html

As Nelson Thornes is not responsible for third party content online, there may be some changes to this material that are beyond our control. In order for us to ensure that the links referred to in the book are as up-to-date and stable as possible, the websites are usually homepages with supporting instructions on how to reach the relevant pages if necessary.

Please let us know at **kerboodle@nelsonthornes.com.** if you find a link that doesn't work and we will do our best to redirect the link, or to find an alternative site.

AQA Information and Communication Technology

A2

Exclusively endorsed by AQA

EHWLC LEARNING CENTRE
EALING GREEN

Diane Spencer
Paul Morgan
Bill Haddock

Series editor
Claire Rees

Nelson Thornes

EG12293

Text © Bill Haddock, Paul Morgan and Diane Spencer 2009
Original illustrations © Nelson Thornes Ltd 2009

The right of Bill Haddock, Paul Morgan and Diane Spencer to be identified as authors of this work has been asserted by them in accordance with the Copyright, Designs and Patents Act 1988.

All rights reserved. No part of this publication may be reproduced or transmitted in any form or by any means, electronic or mechanical, including photocopy, recording or any information storage and retrieval system, without permission in writing from the publisher or under licence from the Copyright Licensing Agency Limited, of Saffron House, 6–10 Kirby Street, London, EC1N 8TS.

Any person who commits any unauthorised act in relation to this publication may be liable to criminal prosecution and civil claims for damages.

Published in 2009 by:
Nelson Thornes Ltd
Delta Place
27 Bath Road
CHELTENHAM
GL53 7TH
United Kingdom

10 11 12 13 / 10 9 8 7 6 5 4 3 2

A catalogue record for this book is available from the British Library

ISBN 978 0 7487 9908 4

Cover photograph: Getty/PNC
Illustrations by Fakenham Photosetting Ltd
Page make-up by Fakenham Photosetting Ltd

Printed in China by 1010 Printing International Ltd

EHWLC LEARNING CENTRE
EALING GREEN

3wk – Main
EG12293
004 SPE

Acknowledgements

The authors and publishers wish to thank the following for permission to use copyright material:

p4, Fig. 1.1.1, Marcus Ward Curran, designer of Eclipse Office Partition System – Digital Hot Desk; p13, Fig. 2.1.1, John Murphy; p24, Fig. 2.4.5, IKEA for material from its website. Copyright © Inter IKEA Systems B.V. 2009; p25, Fig. 2.4.6, PayPal Inc.; p36, Fig. 4.1.2, iStockphoto; p37, Fig. 4.1.3, iStockphoto; Fig. 4.1.4, Fotolia; Fig. 4.1.5, Simon Katzer/Getty Images; p44, Reed Business Information Ltd for an extract from Paul Michaels, 'Calculating the cost of failed software projects', *Computer Weekly*, 31.12.07; p57, Fig. 5.4.2, Fotolia; p70, Wright's Reprints and Incisive Media for an extract from Dave Friedlos, 'Electronic ordering to cut WHSmith's costs' *What PC?*, 22.06.06; p71, Fig. 7.1.1, Connecting for Health. Crown copyright © material is reproduced under Class Licence No. CO1 W 0000195 with the permission of the Controller of HMSO and the Queen's Printer for Scotland; p78, Fig. 7.3.2, Photolibrary; p80, Fig. 7.4.1, Infolock Technologies for material from its website; p91, Fig. 8.2.2, Jim West/Alamy; Fig. 8.2.3, Microsoft product screenshot reprinted with permission from Microsoft Corporation; p92, Fig. 8.2.4, Manor Photography/Alamy; p94, Fig. 8.3.1, Microsoft product screen shot reprinted with permission from Microsoft Corporation; p97, Fig. 8.3.4, Dell Computer Corporation Ltd for material from its website; p98, Fig. 8.4.1, Visual Mining/Alamy; Fig. 8.4.2, Photographers Direct; Fig. 8.4.3, IKEA for material from its website. Copyright © Inter IKEA Systems B.V. 2009; pp104–5, CBS Interactive Ltd for extracts from 'How 9/11 changed disaster planning', www.ZDNet.co.uk, 30.10.06; p108, Fig. 9.3.2, Miray Software AG for material from its website; p110, Fig. 10.1.1, Dave Cameron/Alamy; p111, fig. 10.1.2, Helene Rogers/Alamy; p112, Scientific American Inc. for an extract from Mark Weiser, 'The Computer for the 21st Century', *Scientific American* 265, Nr. 3, S. 94–101. Copyright © 1991 Scientific America, Inc.; p112, Fig. 10.1.4, Optoma UK; p113, Fig. 10.1.3, Uli Nusko/Alamy; p113, Semacode Corporation for material from its website; p115, Fig. 13.1.3, AFP/Getty Images.

Every effort has been made to trace the copyright holders and we apologise if any have been overlooked. Should copyright have been unwittingly infringed in this book, the owners should contact the publishers, who will make corrections at reprint.

Contents

Introduction to this book

This exciting new specification has been designed to meet the needs of students studying ICT in the 21st century. Today's students are digital natives and their expectation of an A Level in ICT is one that will motivate, challenge and excite them; this course aims to do precisely that by encouraging students to become active investigators with a full understanding of when, why and how to use ICT appropriately, fully equipping them for a world beyond their A Level study.

Unit 3: The use of ICT in the digital world examines the implications of continual evolution in technological developments and system capabilities to users of ICT. Specifically, this unit considers the issues associated with managing ICT within this fast-paced world and the role that it plays within organisations, both now and in the future.

Through exploring the use of ICT in supplying information needs, the potential issues surrounding the management of ICT systems and the many factors that determine a company's ICT strategy, students will discover that a company's structure, size or purpose may alter the way that ICT is utilised within the company. Throughout their study, students are encouraged to consider a range of public and private organisations, including small, medium and large businesses, both national and multinational. They should explore a broad variety of business types, including organisations such as clubs and societies, or charities, for example.

A recurring theme through this unit is that each organisation will have different ICT and ICT-management needs to consider. These will include the training and support needed for users of ICT systems within the organisation, the effects of outside organisations on the running of its ICT and the introduction and testing of ICT systems.

Unit 4: INFO4 Practical issues involved in the use of ICT in the digital world is the coursework module for the A Level ICT course. It offers the opportunity for students to prove their transferable skills through the production of an ICT-related system. The coursework will take the form of a substantial project, produced over an extended period of time. It will provide scope for work to be tailored to the individual needs of learners, for groups of students to collaborate, whilst still producing individual work and enable a range of possible projects to be undertaken.

The use of ICT in the digital world

Introduction

This unit is largely concerned with the importance of information to large organisations and how the ICT systems can be used to provide it. It covers the need to produce good quality information for people at all levels in an organization, the role it plays in the decision making process, together with common ICT systems used to support the activities and business goals of that organisation.

ICT strategies are important to the management of all organisations, large and small, but the details of those strategies will vary between organisations. This unit looks at the factors that influence ICT strategy and management and the issues that these strategies relate to. Policies and procedures that ensure the efficient management of resources need to be in place and the impact of legislation on policies and procedures is an important consideration.

The systems development life cycle is used to introduce and maintain ICT systems. This unit explains the need for a systematic, formal approach to development and looks at some of the development methodologies that could be used. Many tools and techniques exist that support the development of ICT solutions and these techniques will also be important in the design and development of coursework projects.

The scale of any ICT development will naturally affect the way it is introduced into to an organisation. Disaster recovery planning is one vital aspect of large scale systems and the need to maintain them is another.

Users of ICT systems will need training of various kinds at intervals during their career and it is important to select an appropriate method of delivery. Options for providing support to users and the factors that might influence the choice of support method are equally important.

Resources and services, both within the organisation and outside it, can be supplied by a variety of methods. Options such as leasing, outsourcing and offshoring are possible but will have implications for organisational management.

And finally – this book does not include a free crystal ball, but it does look at some of the emerging trends in the rapidly changing world of ICT, together with possible implications for individuals, businesses and society.

1 Information

In this section you will cover:

- the information needs of different organisations

- the information needs of different activities within an organisation

- levels of task and their information needs

- information needs of different personnel and exchanging information with them.

AQA Examiner's tip

Probably the most common error that examiners meet is the use of the word 'information' when the correct word would be 'data'. Data is input into an ICT system where it is processed to produce information. Always check your answers to make sure you have chosen the correct word.

As the first section of this course is entitled 'information', it is worth remembering the definition of information as 'Data that has been processed to produce something meaningful'. Most organisations generate a large amount of data from their day-to-day activities and, if they process it effectively, it can produce information that can help them run their activities more effectively. ICT systems can be used to carry out that processing.

1.1 Different organisations have different information needs

Organisations are not necessarily businesses. They can be any group of people who have a common interest – including charities, or public sector organisations such as local authorities or government departments. Schools and colleges are organisations that can be in the public or the private sector and this will affect the way in which they are run and the information that they need to produce. A group of friends who get together to form a dramatic society are still an organisation. All of these organisations need information.

The information needs of organisations will obviously vary depending on their purpose, scale and size. The function of the organisation is the most critical factor – because some small organisations are very dependent on their ICT systems and some large organisations may rely on them less. Large organisations will tend to generate more data, but may not need to process their data in a particularly complex fashion. Public sector organisations are funded by taxpayers and will have to provide very specific information to government bodies about the way they are run. Organisations that rely on large databases or have e-commerce operations are clearly extremely dependent on their ICT systems.

The management style of the organisation will also have an impact. Some organisations like to work at the cutting edge of technology, and will demand highly sophisticated ICT systems, while other organisations

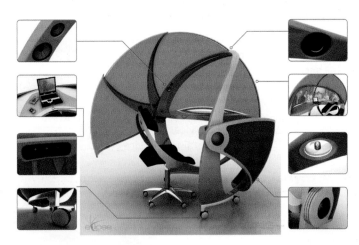

Fig. 1.1.1 *Eclipse Office Partitioning System: for some organisations, a high-tech image is important*

pride themselves on being 'low tech' and prefer to do things in more traditional ways, using computers in only the most basic ways, such as word processing.

Case study: Leatherland

Leatherland is a retail business selling sofas. They have stores across the UK controlled from a head office, where the finance and ICT departments are also based. The company operates in nine regions, each with their own warehouse servicing approximately 10–12 stores. Each store has a manager, sales staff and administration staff. The company uses ICT systems to deal with customer orders and deliveries, manage finance, perform stock control and deliver customer service.

Case study: Oaktree High School

Oaktree High School has 800 pupils on its roll from Year 7 to Year 13. It operates on a single site in a large town. It employs teaching staff, administration staff and support staff such as librarians, technicians, maintenance staff and cleaners. Catering is contracted out to a local company.

It uses a management information system (MIS) to produce information about student performance, sets and timetables, registration, finance and ordering and examination entries. It employs a network manager plus an ICT technician.

1.2 Different activities within an organisation have different information needs

Within any organisation, some departments may well use ICT more than others. Most organisations that pay employees use payroll software that helps them calculate salaries and wages, together with the deductions they have to make for national insurance and income tax. Finance departments can also use accounting and financial modelling software to track income and expenditure and plan for the future.

Retail organisations need to order products from wholesalers and suppliers and manufacturing organisations need to order the raw materials that they use to make their products. They could use the Internet to search for suppliers and may well use ICT systems to order the goods they need. Holding stock is expensive and many organisations operate a '**just in time**' policy that relies heavily on information from ICT systems. Materials are ordered so that they arrive just in time to be used in the manufacturing process and companies use sophisticated production control software that makes sure that materials do not run out. Information is exchanged with suppliers and customers through a computer-based system that sends data directly between computer systems. It uses agreed formats that avoid data having to be re-entered and so eliminates data entry errors and reduces delivery times.

> ## Key terms
>
> **Just in time manufacturing:** uses computer systems to ensure raw process and stock levels are kept to a minimum.

■ Case study: Oaktree High School

Ordering supplies

The Oaktree High School's management system is also used to order goods from suppliers. Each member of staff is issued with a personalised login and they can order the goods that they need from the websites of approved suppliers. Orders are authorised by the bursar and passed directly to the suppliers using **EDI**. The details of the order only need to be entered once, reducing the chances of data entry errors. Payments are authorised by the school and the money is transferred to the supplier's account via **BACS** – the Bankers Automated Clearing Service – which is another example of EDI. The main disadvantage is that it becomes more difficult to order from suppliers who are not part of the system.

Fig. 1.2.1 *BACS: Using EDI and BACS makes school ordering more efficient*

■ Key terms

EDI (Electronic Data Interchange): sends data in agreed formats between computer applications in different organisations.

BACS: The Bankers Automated Clearing Service is a method of processing financial transactions electronically.

■ Case study: Leatherland

Customer support

Leatherland's service manager and reporting system logs complaints from customers and categorises them depending on whether they concern poor service, late delivery, manufacturing defects etc. Complaints are investigated and dealt with and, if necessary, refunds are arranged for the customer.

Complaints are monitored closely and the system produces reports about any patterns in complaints, perhaps from a particular store or about goods from a particular upholsterer. If the complaints are not dealt with quickly, they are flagged by the system as needing urgent attention.

■ End of sub-topic questions

1 Many business organisations adopt a 'just in time' stock control and ordering policy. Explain what this means, why they do this and how ICT can help them to achieve it.

1.3 Different levels of task have different information needs

Most organisations have a hierarchy, which means that staff operate at different levels of responsibility and the tasks they perform can be considered to be at three levels.

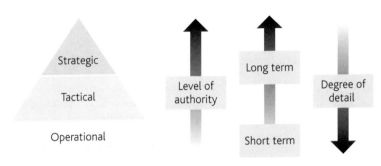

Fig. 1.3.1 *Levels of task within organisations*

Operational level tasks are the everyday tasks that keep an organisation operating. Tactical and strategic levels of task are concerned with managing the activities of the organisation.

	Operational	Tactical	Strategic
Type of decision	Structured	Semi-structured	Unstructured
Effect	Short term	Medium term	Long term
Degree of detail needed	Detailed	Some summary	Summarised

In the case of Leatherland, the operational level staff would be the sales assistants, administrators and delivery drivers. The decisions they take are fairly routine, such as how much to charge a customer, how much a sales assistant has earned this month, which is the best route to a customer's house. These types of decisions, which follow a clear set of rules, are called structured decisions. They are easy to automate in systems such as EPOS tills and payroll software. Their decisions take immediate effect and require information in considerable detail.

Tactical level staff would be store managers and senior administrators. The decisions they take do not follow such straightforward rules; they are semi-structured and the manager has more control over what happens. An example might be whether extending opening hours would justify the increased cost by generating extra sales. They affect the medium term operation of the organisation. The information required at this level needs to be summarised rather than in great detail. The manager of a store wants to be able to judge how each sales assistant is performing and how well the store is doing overall. They do not need to see every order in the detail that a sales assistant would need. Good quality information can make tactical decisions much easier.

The strategic level is the highest in the organisation and the decisions at this level affect the way the organisation moves forward in the long term.

These decisions are complex and lack structure. There may be no single right answer and the information needed to make these decisions may come from many sources, both within and outside the organisation. In the case of Leatherland, most strategic decision making will take place by senior managers at head office. A decision to extend the product range to take in other types of furniture, for example, would be a strategic one. The directors would need to see summarised reports on many different aspects of the performance of the company and its competitors before reaching a decision.

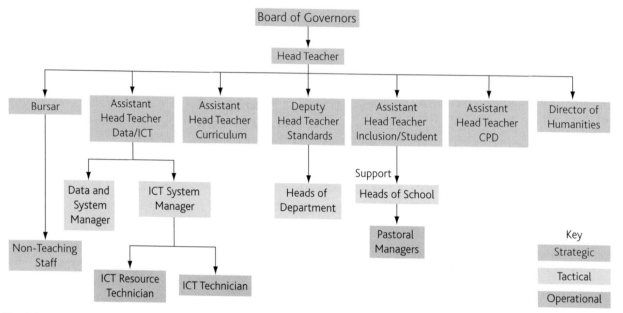

Fig. 1.3.2 *Organisational chart for Oaktree High School*

Activity

Look at the diagram for the large school shown above. Think about your own school or college. Which job roles do you think are operational and which are tactical and strategic? Remember that one person may have more than one role in the organisation. A head of department may also be a teacher, a head of year, a member of the pastoral committee and a teacher governor.

Give examples of tasks that are carried out at each level and decisions that are made.

End of sub-topic questions

2   A sports centre collects data about its members when they enrol. Each time they use the centre for any activity, their membership card is scanned to register for that specific activity in that session.

a   What data is collected when the member registers for an activity?

b   This data is then processed to produce information that is used at the operational level. Give an example of a task that is carried out at the operational level and what information might be useful for it.

c   This data can be processed further to provide useful information at the tactical and strategic levels. Explain this, giving examples of information that might be produced.

1.4 Different personnel have different information needs

As well as the people working in an organisation, it is likely that people outside the organisation will need information from it, and there are many methods of achieving this, depending on the style of the organisation and the technology available.

Suppliers

Suppliers will need to know details of the materials the organisation needs to order and how they are going to be paid for. Simple products such as office supplies may be ordered through the supplier's website. The goods may be paid for using a credit or debit card, or the supplier may send an invoice which is paid later, usually within 30 days. In order to do this, the organisation will have to set up an account with the supplier. They will then be supplied with a user name and password in order to maintain security and prevent unauthorised orders.

Large organisations may have an extranet, which enables suppliers to log in to their network. Obviously, their access will be limited to the parts that they need. The school management system described above may be an example of this.

In addition to these formal communication methods, customers and suppliers will also communicate less formally via e-mail and telephone, but many suppliers will insist on written orders, usually with purchase order numbers, so that both parties are agreed as to what will be supplied and when. Financial information is better dealt with through more secure methods that have encryption built in.

Customers

The above methods are also available for organisations to deal with their customers, along with:

- Website FAQs can be useful to deal with the questions that organisations are often asked. The customer may be able to find the answer quickly and it is efficient because no staff time is used up, except for the time spent setting up the FAQs themselves. This method is very impersonal and limited to those customers who have Internet access.

- E-mail allows the company to answer the customer personally (although standard replies that are in many ways similar to FAQ responses may be used). They are not as personal as a telephone call, but they do avoid the customer having to wait in a phone queue, and they give the customer support team time to investigate the problem and respond appropriately. They also allow the workload to be smoothed out, as they do not have to be dealt with instantly in the way that a phone call does.

- Internet chat is becoming a popular way of dealing with customer queries. Customers indicate on the company website that they wish to speak to an advisor and are placed in a queue for a private chat room. The service uses instant messaging technology so the customer types in their questions and the advisor responds in the same way. The advisor often looks up the answers to queries on a knowledge base system and makes that available to the customer, rather than having to type out a long and complex explanation. This does mean that the customer avoids waiting in a phone queue – they can simply keep an eye on their screen to see when they are coming to the top of the queue. This method has the advantage of providing a written record of the discussion – useful to refer back to later, especially if there is a dispute about what has been said.

On many company websites it is probably true to say that the hardest piece of information to find is a contact telephone number. Other methods of customer support tend to be cheaper to manage and many companies will try to avoid telephone calls as far as they can. Many customers, however, still prefer to talk to a real person!

Official and legal bodies

Many organisations have to deal with official bodies such as the Inland Revenue (the government department dealing with income tax) and HM Revenue and Customs (who deal with company registrations, corporation tax and VAT). They may also have to register company vehicles with the DVLA or work with agencies helping people with disabilities.

The Directgov website (www.direct.gov.uk) is a web portal site that links to a number of government agencies. Each agency then has its own website so, for instance when a company needs to post its annual accounts, it can do so directly on the website. They will be issued with security codes to ensure that only the appropriate people have access.

Activity

Look at the Directgov website. Make a list of some of the government agencies that an organisation (rather than an individual) might have to exchange information with and what information would be involved.

1.5 Exchange of information with external bodies

When communicating with any external body, an organisation has to ensure that it complies with privacy, security and legal requirements.

The Data Protection Act, for example, controls who personal data can be passed on to, and organisations must ensure they only pass on data in accordance with their registration at the Information Commission. They also have to make sure the data is kept secure, and that might involve encrypting the data as it is being exchanged.

If a company operates an e-commerce site it has to protect the financial details of its customers so that, when financial details are processed, the data is encrypted and customer credit details are never stored in a form that would make them accessible and usable for fraudulent purposes. Some businesses use an intermediate service such as PayPal so that they do not have to deal directly with customers' credit cards and the security is handled for them.

Did you know?

There have been several well-publicised cases of data being posted to other parts of the country on removable media such as CDRs, which have been lost in transit. EDI would be a safer method of doing this. If using removable media is the only way of transporting the data, then the data should be encrypted so that if it goes missing it cannot easily be read without the decryption key, which is unlikely to be available. Of course, sensitive data should always be encrypted, however it is being transferred.

Activity

Look at two e-commerce sites operated by large online retailers. There should be a statement to reassure shoppers about the security of their data. Summarise the security precautions that the organisations have in place in the form of a digital poster.

End of sub-topic questions

3 Moody Sports is a wholesaler who sells clothing and equipment to schools and colleges. It has to exchange information with many different bodies. Describe three organisations with which Moody Sports needs to exchange information, giving examples of the information that might be involved. Explain to Rob, the owner, why setting up EDI arrangements might be beneficial to his business.

✓ *In this section you have covered:*

- the fact that organisations can be of different types, e.g. public bodies or private businesses

- organisations also vary in scale. Large organisations will tend to have more data but their information needs may not always be complex. That will depend on what their function is

- people in the organisation carry out tasks at operational, tactical and strategic levels

- at the higher levels, decisions will be less structured. Operational level tasks are sometimes automated

- the need for organisations to exchange data and information with suppliers, customers and official bodies

- the methods they may use to do this, via websites, extranets, EDI and e-mail

- the need to maintain security and privacy of data when it is transferred.

Systems

2.1 The role of ICT in organisations

In Section 1 we established that an organisation was a group of people with a common purpose. Any organisation will have aims. Without them, there is no point in having an organisation. Some business organisations have a mission statement, which is more or less permanently fixed. Its aims will be long term, but will change over time.

Activity

Look on websites or in company literature to find the aims of some organisations. Choose a variety – some public sector, some private, some large organisations and some small. If the organisation has a mission statement, make a note of that too. How do the aims and mission statement relate to one another?

The role of ICT in any organisation is to help it to achieve its aims efficiently and effectively. How it does this will vary a great deal between one organisation and another. Some will use ICT to design and produce things, and some to sell things. Other organisations will use ICT mostly for administration, to keep track of finances and employee records. Some organisations produce ICT-based products such as software or websites.

ICT equipment can be an expensive investment and the cost of it needs to be justified in financial terms against the benefits it brings. The costs involved are not just those of hardware and software as large systems will need network managers, technicians and ICT support staff, all of whom have to be paid.

So how can ICT systems justify their cost?

Remember

ICT systems are those where the output from the system goes directly to a human being or into another ICT system. They have three basic stages, input, processing and output. They are made up of people, data, procedures, software, hardware and information.

- they may save time compared to manual methods. Imagine if supermarkets had to go back to manual cash registers, where the checkout operator had to know the price of each product and enter it manually into the till! EPOS systems move customers through more quickly, so fewer checkout operators are needed for the same volume of sales. This saves the supermarket money

- they may help the company to produce a better product. Computer-aided design means that an architect can design a building in two dimensions and view it in three dimensions. He can change the materials, add or remove features and experiment until it looks right. He then has the ability to superimpose the building on a picture of its proposed location and even create the ability to 'walk' around it to see what it would look like. A client would find it much easier to imagine the buildings like this than from traditional architect's plans and changes can be made at this modelling stage much more easily than on a completed building! The drawing below uses a mixture of standard shapes and rendered drawings to give visual information about the proposed development to the client.

- ICT systems may save money by estimating materials and timing more accurately than can be achieved by other methods. The CAD software used by the architect can calculate how many bricks need

Fig. 2.1.1 *This new development is much easier to visualise in three dimensions than in two*

to be ordered, how many light fittings will be needed and how much concrete it will take to create the foundations. Project management software can be used to plan when all of those materials need to be on site so that the builders are not waiting around, but avoiding expensive materials being stored and perhaps even stolen.

Senior management needs to identify **Critical Success Factors** (CSF), the elements or activities that are vital to the success of the business, and then put information systems in place to support each of these CSFs.

 Activity

Look again at the aims of the organisations you listed in the first activity. Using two different examples, find out what you can from their corporate website or other sources about the way they use ICT systems to achieve their aims.

 PC activity

Design an ICT system that will enable a teacher at Oakwood School to keep track of class work and homework marks over half a term and then produce a simple personalised report for each pupil.

 End of sub-topic questions

1 Oakwood School's aim is 'To treat all our pupils as individuals and help them to achieve their maximum potential'.

Explain how the school can use ICT to track the achievements and performance of each of its pupils in order to meet its aims.

Key terms

Critical Success Factors (CSF): the essential areas of activity that must be performed well if the objectives or goals of an organisation or project are to be achieved.

Key terms

Payroll: the administration of wages and salaries.

Human resources (HR): the department that deals with the management of the people who work for an organisation. Sometimes it is called the personnel department.

AQA Examiner's tip

Payroll systems can be extremely complex and the rules for them change with each government budget and so they should be treated with caution when you are choosing a suitable project for this A Level.

Did you know?

The BCS (British Computer Society) produces the Skills Framework for the Information Age. SFIA is the high-level UK Government-backed competency framework describing the roles within IT and the skills needed to fulfil them. These can be linked into HR systems to provide a consistent structure on which to base ICT appointments.

The website www.bcs.org gives further details – follow the link to 'Professional Development'.

2.2 Common ICT systems used in organisations

Most organisations use ICT to some extent in their administration processes. Some of the most commonly used systems are:

- payroll
- accounting
- human resource management.

Payroll systems, as the name suggests, calculate wages and salaries. Special purpose software can be purchased off the shelf and then configured to meet the needs of the organisation. These calculations are quite complex as they need to deduct the correct amounts for income tax, national insurance and pension contributions. They need to keep track of each employee's payments and the amounts the organisation needs to pay to government bodies such as the Inland Revenue. The rules for the amount to be deducted will depend on the circumstances and the rules set by the government. These rules change from time to time, and most software will need to be modified regularly by downloading updates from the software company's website. The software will have features built in to produce the required documents, such as personalised wage slips for each employee and a P60 form to sum up an employee's record at the end of each tax year. The system has to be subject to audit – a mechanism to prove that the calculations have been carried out in accordance with the law.

Accounting systems manage the financial operations of a business or organisation. They can help to keep track of expenditure by setting up cost centres or budgets for various departments and monitoring expenditure against them. They can also deal with invoicing and payments and keep track of assets and their values.

Human Resources, or Personnel, departments store data about the people who work for the organisation, and are based around powerful databases. Some packages are purchased in modules so that organisations only need to buy the ones that suit their own operations. The basic module would store personal data such as contact details and date of appointment, plus records of promotions and any disciplinary incidents. Other modules might track skills and training. The software will have powerful reporting options so that, for instance, if a vacancy arose needing a specific set of skills, the database could produce a list of people who ought to be considered.

Some software houses sell software that can perform all of these administration functions. It is generally sold on a modular basis, so a company can choose what they need. This has the major advantage that the various modules link together and so queries can be performed across the full range of data available without having to re-enter data to carry out the analysis. For example, the company could conduct some analysis as to whether the level of training of staff affected their sales figures and contribution to profits. They could then build a financial model to investigate the cost benefit of investing more in training programmes. Data about employees, for example, would be common to the HR and payroll systems, making the whole system more efficient than would be the case if separate packages were purchased.

There is a need for data to be transferred between ICT systems both internally and externally. If the internal systems are linked in the way described above, then the transfer becomes very simple. Even if the software is not part of the same suite, it may still be possible to export

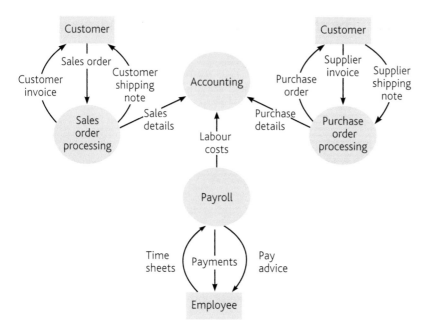

Fig. 2.2.1 *Systems diagram of main components of business systems*

data directly in a format that is suitable for importing to a second package.

No organisation can exist in isolation; there is also a need for information to be transferred between the organisations ICT systems and the ICT systems of external agencies. These external agencies have their own information requirements so that they can carry out their own functions.

A wholesale organisation will need to transfer information to and from suppliers and retailers in order to maintain its supply chain. The supplier needs to know what the wholesaler needs so that they can supply it, and the retailer needs to know what goods they will receive and when they will arrive so that they know what stock they have available to sell.

At Leatherland (Case study 1) information is transferred from its sales and invoicing system to the furniture manufacturers so that the correct furniture is delivered at the right time to the right distribution warehouse.

A school, or college, (such as Case study 2) exchanges information with external agencies such as examination boards. Most exam entries are sent directly from the school's system by Electronic Data Interchange (EDI), to the exam board's information system. Exam results are sent back to the school by the same method.

All organisations will need to transfer information between themselves and government agencies, e.g. for tax purposes. The Inland Revenue need to know how much each employee has been paid so that they can check that the correct amount of income tax is paid.

When data needs to be transferred between systems, EDI is the most efficient method if it is available.

It goes without saying that the ICT systems of any organisation must meet the demands of the organisation itself. These will vary depending on the activities with which the organisation is involved.

2.3 The requirements of external agencies

Supply chain

The links between the raw materials from which products are made and the customers who purchase them are known as the supply chain and can be very complex. Consider a sofa made mostly from leather and wood:

1 The leather starts off as the skin of an animal on a farm, the wood as a tree in a forest.
2 These goods are passed to processors who turn them into leather and timber.
3 The furniture manufacturer purchases those goods and builds them into a sofa.
4 Leatherland purchase many sofas and distribute them to their warehouses.
5 A customer orders their sofa from a shop.
6 The shop contacts the warehouse and arranges for the sofa to be delivered to the customer.

And that ignores the foam, nails, springs, glues and other materials that will also be needed!

The supply chain needs to be maintained smoothly, because a delay anywhere in that system can mean that the customer does not get their goods when they want them and is likely to cancel their order and buy from somewhere else. No organisation in the chain wants to hold large amounts of stock because that ties up finance and they may be left with unwanted stock as fashions change and customers require different designs. Good communications are vital so that customers are quoted realistic deliveries that can be achieved in practice. These must not be too long, however, or the customer will simply shop elsewhere.

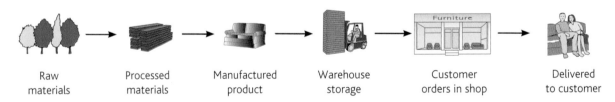

| Raw materials | Processed materials | Manufactured product | Warehouse storage | Customer orders in shop | Delivered to customer |

Fig. 2.3.1 *A delay anywhere in the supply chain will affect delivery time to the customer*

Legacy systems

When an organisation invests in a new ICT system it may not replace every part of the system and some older 'legacy' systems may still be used. In this case, it is essential that **data portability** is maintained. This means that data can be transferred between the old and new systems electronically, whenever it needs to be, without being re-entered.

If the legacy system is to be totally replaced by the new one, then **data transferability** is important. This means that data from the old system can be imported into the new system when the new system is being installed.

Key terms

Data portability: the ability to transfer data between different software packages or systems.

Data transferability: the ability to import data from an old ICT system to a new one when the new one is being installed.

End of sub-topic questions

2 State three external organisations that would receive information from a school and for each, give an example of the information that would be passed on.

3 Give three examples of information a school would receive from external organisations and, for each one, state its source.

4 Sometimes, information might have to be output as hard copy from one organisation's ICT system, transferred to an external organisation and entered manually into their ICT system. Describe two problems that may be caused by this procedure.

AQA Examiner's tip

Where the question says 'describe', make sure you give enough detail in your answer. One word answers or short phrases will not be sufficient to gain the marks.

2.4 Types of ICT system and their uses

Just as tasks can be divided into strategic, tactical and operational levels, the ICT systems that support them can be divided in a similar way. Operational level systems, sometimes called data processing systems, are the ones that carry out the repetitive, low-level tasks that keep organisations running on a day-to-day basis. Tactical level systems summarise that data for middle managers in order to give them information to help them make the decisions they need to run the organisation in the medium term. That data is further summarised, together with data from outside the organisation, to help senior managers at tactical level make the big decisions that control the long term future of the organisation.

Back office systems

The term 'back office' comes from the usual layout of the building of early companies. The front office would contain the sales and other customer-facing staff and the back office would be where staff carried out the manufacturing or developing of products, or were involved in administration. The term '**back office systems**' has come to mean the ICT systems that run the internal operations of an organisation that are not accessible or visible to the general public.

Transaction processing systems

Transaction processing systems are used at the operational level of organisations. Much of the day-to-day business of any organisation can be considered as a series of simple transactions. These might be commercial transactions, such as withdrawing money from an ATM, buying a train ticket or paying a bill. Others involve recording or retrieving data (making a booking, enrolling a student at university or looking up examination results).

Each transaction is in itself quite simple; in an EPOS system a bar code is scanned, the product number is used to look up the item description, its price and any special offers that might apply, the receipt is printed and payment is recorded. However, in most organisations, there are very large numbers of these transactions – so the speed and efficiency of carrying out these transactions is an important consideration. Automatic data capture methods such as reading bar codes are generally worthwhile investments because they speed up data capture and have built-in validation to reduce data entry errors.

The data recorded by the transaction processing systems can then be passed on into other systems within the organisation. The supermarket will use its checkout data for stock control, financial management,

Key terms

Back office systems: the ICT systems that run the internal operations of an organisation and are not accessible or visible to the general public.

Transaction processing systems: these carry out the day-to-day activities of most organisations at operational level.

analysis of checkout operator performance and many other functions at tactical and strategic levels.

Case study: payroll system

A weekly payroll system produces two primary outputs – the amount to be paid to each employee and a printed record (pay advice) of the payments made. The payments are the basic transactions of this system.

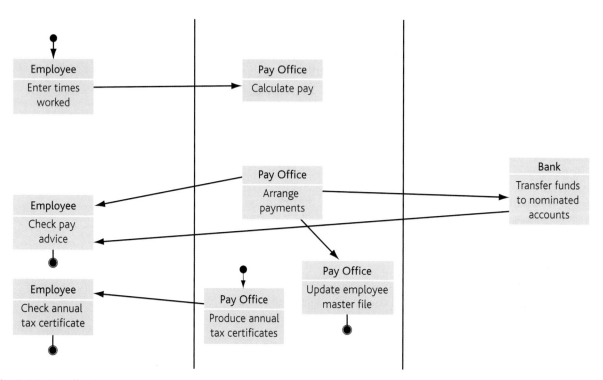

Fig. 2.4.1 *Payroll system*

The main data inputs are the employee ID and hours worked that week for each person.

The payroll system may interact with the accounting or HR system, in order to look up the other details, such as rate of pay, tax code, employee name that it needs in order to produce the pay advice. It will then produce details of the bank account details and amount to be paid to each person so that this can be transferred to the employee's account by BACS.

Other outputs of the system include the tax certificates sent annually to employees and the Inland Revenue. Each department will also be allocated a cost centre code and reports for managers, showing the payments made to staff against these codes will be produced by the software. These reports to managers are an important control in the system, as the cost centre managers should detect any invalid payments when reviewing them.

Another control would be the employees themselves, who are likely to complain if their pay is significantly different from what they were expecting.

Workflow systems

Workflow management systems use ICT to manage business processes. The software helps organisations to define and analyse their business processes and to identify possible problem areas that are slowing down the information flow and affecting the efficiency of the complete system. Once the optimum workflow routes have been established, the software allows the user to design forms that collect data efficiently and automatically pass it on to the appropriate destinations. Because the process is centrally controlled, it makes tracking work much more efficient and the position of any particular job within the system can be traced. Powerful reporting facilities enable managers to assess the current situation and model future progress. It also provides information that can help them improve the situation, perhaps by re-allocating team members to different tasks to clear a backlog that is holding things up. Workflow systems often include document management systems.

Key terms

Workflow management system: software that helps organisations analyse and manage their business processes by using a computer model to represent the logic of the workflow.

Case study: loan company

A UK-based loans company decided it needed to improve the efficiency of its applications process, which was initially paper-based.

Before

The system used by this company for approving loans was paper-based. If a department wanted to work on the application, they

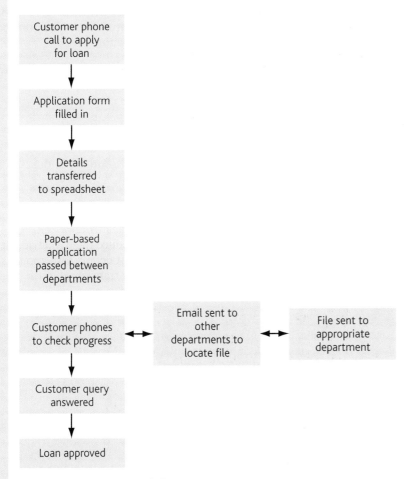

Fig. 2.4.2 *Loan company – before new system*

e-mailed other departments and the paper file was passed on. The system was slow, it generated lots of e-mail traffic and the customer had to wait if they wanted to check how their application was going.

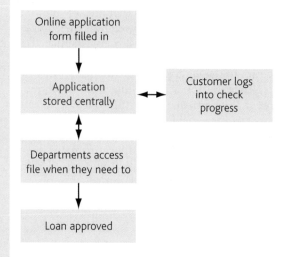

Fig. 2.4.3 *Loan company – after new system*

After

The customer makes an online application via the website and is issued with a customer ID and password that they can use to find out the status of their application. All departments can access centrally-stored electronic files, ensuring that they are all working on the most up-to-date version of the application.

The new system has doubled the number of loans the company can process in a single day.

▓ Did you know?

The Microsoft website (www.microsoft.com) has more case studies on this and other topics. Follow the link to the case studies.

CASE (Computer Aided Software Engineering) tools can be used in the creation of workflow-based applications. IBM's 'WebSphere Process Modeler' and 'Websphere Workflow' packages are examples of this.

This type of software enables the user to produce graphical process diagrams of those activities, which can then be run in order to look for problems. The user:

- defines activities
- allocates staff to those activities
- defines organisations
- allocates staff to organisations
- attaches programs to activities.

An animated simulation of the processes and activities can then be run so that the designer can identify problem areas and bottlenecks, perhaps reallocating staff to smooth out the process.

Document management systems

Document management systems were originally developed to store paper based documents electronically. Documents were scanned and stored as picture files, with keywords, authors and other data relating to the document recorded, very much like a library system. Using this system documents were much easier to search for and retrieve than they would have been in a paper based system. As more documents were produced electronically systems developed so that they could also be stored and tracked in an electronic archive for easy retrieval. **Metadata** from the document contents is searchable in a similar way to conducting a browser search on the web and combinations of keywords, dates and any other criteria specified by the user are used to track down the right document. OCR technology is now used to convert paper based documents and forms into electronic ones, although handwritten documents need to be written on special forms if they are to be scanned in this way. These systems can be used to store and track business documents, academic papers or historical records at archive centres such as libraries.

Systems for collaborative working

When teams of people are working on a single project, they often need to access and update project documents. The control of this can be a major problem, as there is a danger that two people will each load a document and make changes to it, meaning that there are several versions in existence and some people will be working from the wrong version. Version control is difficult to achieve, but is vital to avoid mistakes and wasted time. Systems should be set up so that only one member of the team can have ownership of a document at any one time, and they are the only person allowed to make changes to it. When they have finished with it, they update the version number and send the new version to other members of the team, who then use the new one. In practice, this seldom works, because people forget to check for the latest version. A better method is to set up a shared space, sometimes called a document repository or an e-room. Documents are uploaded to this central space and if a member of the team wishes to make changes to a document, they have to check it out, just like a book in a library. They then have ownership of that document until they check it back in. If other team members wish to view that document, they may be able to, but the system will warn them that it is checked out to someone else and so it may change. The system automatically updates the version number when the document is checked in. This system, like most others, only works as long as people follow the procedures and don't save local copies of the document on their own computer. Providing that they always go back to the central area, they should be working from the most up-to date version of the document they need.

Key terms

Metadata: data about data. It provides information about the content of documents using key words, descriptions and dates.

Case study: e-room

This book has been written by a team of authors and editors. Each section is written by an author and uploaded to an Internet-based e-room. The first person who needs to review the section has to check out the document and can then add comments or make changes using reviewing tools such as track changes. They then upload the new version and the system gives it a new date and version number. While the document is checked out, other people can read it but not make changes to it, thus ensuring that only one version of the document exists at any one time and people are not wasting time working on out-of-date documents.

The author then checks out the documents, reads the comments and makes the necessary changes. Other reviewers will repeat the process of adding comments until the final version of the document is agreed and it is handed over for printing.

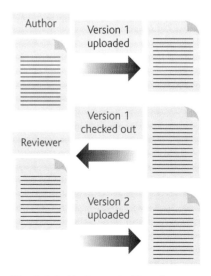

Fig. 2.4.4 *Version control is easier to maintain through a central e-room document repository*

These systems may also have other features, such as a message board where people can leave comments for others to see or a private discussion area for instant message chat between members of the team. It may also allow the team to hold virtual meetings using video or audio conferencing facilities. The person running the meeting can work through a script, releasing documents at appropriate times and gathering in responses from other team members who could be anywhere in the world.

Some systems allow one person to take over another's desktop remotely, which can be useful during training sessions to show someone how to do something.

Activity

The website www.gotomeeting.com gives an overview of one company's online meeting software, including a demonstration and some case studies.

Click on the 'Watch Demo' link on the 'How It Works' page.

Watch the presentation about online meeting software and then write a brief report summing up its advantages and disadvantages compared with other methods that the sales team could use to share information.

Management Information Systems (MIS)

Key terms

Management Information System (MIS): takes data from internal and external sources and processes it to provide information that can be used by managers at different levels to aid effective decision making.

A **Management Information System (MIS)** is a system that converts data from internal and external sources into information. This information is communicated in an appropriate form at an appropriate time to managers at different levels who use the information produced to enable them to make effective decisions for controlling and managing the company.

The data that is produced by the lower levels of the organisation all feed into the management information system and is analysed to produce information that can be used at strategic and tactical levels of the organisation. The strength of a good MIS is that the data from the various sources is summarised and presented in forms that are easy for managers to interpret. One technique that is used is that of exception reporting, where the presentation makes it obvious where there are problems. For example, if a chain store has 35 branches and 33 of them are meeting their targets, the focus needs to be on the two that are failing. The MIS allows the senior manager to look more closely at those stores by drilling down into the data and analysing their performance across a range of criteria. They may also examine available information on competitor performance for shops in that area. Ultimately, strategic level managers will need to make a decision on whether the failing stores are to be kept open, and so having good quality information is vitally important.

It is worth remembering that collecting and analysing data to produce information at this level can be expensive and the cost has to be justified in terms of cost savings or improved performance.

Case study: stock control MIS

A company took over the catering operation for a large city theatre. In their first Christmas pantomime season, they totally underestimated the amount of soft drinks that they would need compared to wine and other alcoholic beverages. Wholesalers tend to be closed over the Christmas period and the stock control manager was reduced to rushing around small local shops to buy whatever stock he could, paying a much higher price than he would have done from the wholesaler.

The sales figures for that year were fed into the stock control system and the following year they would be able to view the previous year's figures in order to decide what to order for that year. They would also be able to view the relative sales of various choices in the restaurant in order to decide which combinations of dishes would prove most popular and profitable at different times of year.

Decision Support Systems (DSS)

Decision support systems are refined Management Information Systems designed to help senior managers to make strategic decisions by providing useful information. DSS systems are intended to be interactive, to allow managers to use data from a variety of sources, extracting information that will help them with the decision making process. There are many types of DSS, operating in many different fields.

Expert systems are one example of a DSS, and are based on artificial intelligence techniques. These systems make use of a knowledge base that is interpreted using a set of rules. Some of these rules are heuristic rules – they are not devised purely from logic, but also from the experience of a person. They attempt to replicate the knowledge of a human expert. As new problems are discovered and solved, the rules are added to the knowledge base and made available in future searches. The user can query the data using a user-friendly interface.

Enterprise systems

Enterprise systems are most often seen in large and medium sized organisations. They aim to overcome the difficulties caused by different systems being run in different departments or businesses within a very large organisation. An enterprise system is typically based on a very large database, which may be extremely complex in structure. Enterprise systems are expensive to set up and maintain, requiring powerful servers and good communication links, but they do ensure that all parts of the organisation are working with the best information the organisation can provide. **Data mining** techniques can be used to look for hidden patterns in the data that may be useful and not immediately obvious.

Customer Relationship Management (CRM)

Customers are obviously an extremely important part of any business and customer relationship management software can be used to store data about customers in order to improve the service that customer receives and increase the likelihood of repeat business. A customer's account may be handled by many different departments within an organisation but it is frustrating for the customer if they are directed to one department after another, each perhaps only having part of the picture. CRM software stores the customer data centrally so that the up-to-date information is available to all departments.

Key terms

Decision Support Systems: computer-based systems that analyse data to provide information to help managers make decisions.

Enterprise systems: those that serve the enterprise as a whole rather than any individual department.

Data mining: the extraction of previously unknown and potentially useful information from data.

Remember

The website www.atwebo.com/dss_examples.htm#DSS%20EXAMPLES gives examples of decision support systems.

Did you know?

When one large supermarket carried out a data mining exercise they found an unexpected rise in the sale of beer and of disposable nappies, with the same customers buying both at about 5.30 p.m. Further investigation showed men were being asked to pick up nappies on their way home from work and the beer mysteriously found its way into the trolley too. Moving displays of premium beers closer to the nappies created an increase in premium beer sales as opposed to the cheaper brands that were purchased previously.

Customer data can be analysed and grouped into categories to indicate who is most likely to bring in profitable business, and the efforts of the organisation can be directed towards those customers. Banks, for example, make money from selling financial products to business customers and individuals and CRM software will indicate likely candidates for mortgage, pension and insurance business.

A **data warehouse** can be used to store the vast quatitities of data generated by enterprise ECRM systems.

E-commerce

With the increased accessibility of fast Internet access, many organisations have adopted the use of e-commerce to buy and sell their goods and services. Most of the transactions are carried out directly through websites, although some organisations still use their website just as an advertising method and customers still do the actual ordering by post or over the phone. Furthermore, it is worth considering that some customers do not have credit or debit cards and need to be able to send their payment by cheque rather than paying online. Organisations that do not utilise e-commerce are now becoming fewer, however.

The most efficient way is a professionally designed **e-commerce system** where a customer can browse for the goods they want, check stock availability, place their order and pay for their goods there and then. If they are buying electronic products, such as software, music or clip art, they may also be able to download the actual product from the website immediately. E-tickets can also be delivered electronically. Motor vehicle, TV and even fishing licences can also be purchased online, avoiding the long queues that used to develop at post offices to obtain them.

The IKEA website gives customers lots of useful information (see Figure 2.4.5).

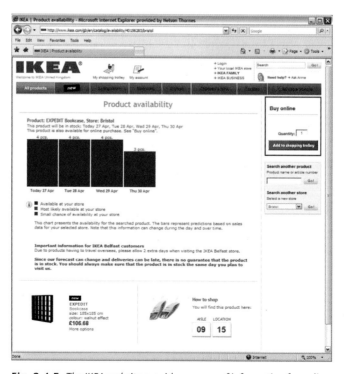

Fig. 2.4.5 *The IKEA website provides a range of information for online and store-based shoppers*

Key terms

Data warehouse: a storage facility for large quantities of data.

E-commerce system: designed to support the buying and selling of goods and services, usually over the World Wide Web.

Activity

Customer relationship management

A large bank allocates customer relationship managers to all clients with above-average incomes.

Discuss in pairs:

■ what information the customer relations manager needs to be available when he or she meets a customer

■ the sources of the data that will be processed to produce that information.

Some retailers, such as Amazon, are purely e-commerce operations and have been since they began. Others combine a 'bricks and mortar' operation with online sales and most established high street retailers also have an e-commerce operation. Many give the customer the option of ordering their goods online and then collecting them from their local store. This means the customer avoids having to visit the store to choose their item and check if it is in stock, then queuing to pay for it. They simply turn up at the store with a printed receipt and the card they used to pay for it with and the goods should be waiting for them. This avoids payment of delivery charges and the customer's need to wait in for deliveries, which can be drawbacks of online shopping. It also means that customers can choose their goods at whatever time is convenient.

The security of online financial transactions is obviously vital and is a cause for concern for many potential customers. Secure servers need to be set up so that all financial transactions are encrypted and these websites display an **https** rather than the usual **http** in their URL. A padlock symbol is also displayed to make customers aware of the security that is in place. Organisations have to be approved by their bank before they can offer this service and customer payments are protected against fraud.

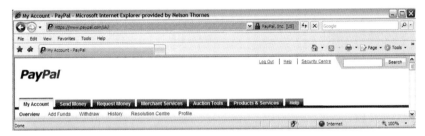

Fig. 2.4.6 *This payment website uses https and displays the padlock symbol to show it is secure*

The requirements of small businesses and individuals buying and selling on online auctions sites can be met by intermediary banking organisations such as PayPal. The customer and the supplier each set up accounts which link to their bank account or credit card. PayPal actually deals with the transfer of funds, so the customer's bank details do not need to be passed on directly to the supplier. Their fee is usually paid by the supplier, who builds it into their pricing.

E-commerce does have its drawbacks. Fraudulent companies can be set up who send goods of extremely poor quality, if they send the goods at all. They move on quickly, setting up a new website before they can be traced and prosecuted. These organisations are often linked with spam e-mail and phishing frauds that attempt to obtain people's bank details under false pretences. Also, it is impossible to try on clothes or find out how comfortable a piece of furniture is until the goods are delivered and, if they are unsuitable, the customer may have to pay return delivery costs. Delivery costs can be high and it may not be convenient to be at home when the delivery arrives. Furthermore, many people shop as a social or leisure activity, enjoying the opportunity to browse, perhaps as part of an afternoon out with friends or family.

☑ *In this section you have covered:*

- the fact that an organisation's ICT strategy must be designed to help it achieve its aims
- the use of ICT applications in the areas of payroll, accounting and personnel management
- back office systems
- transaction processing systems; workflow and document management systems; systems for collaborative working
- management information systems (MIS)
- enterprise systems
- customer relationship management systems
- decision support systems (DSS)
- e-commerce.

💡 3.1 ICT management styles

It is true to say that large organisations tend to have more formal structures than smaller ones. There is an old party game called Chinese Whispers where one person whispers a phrase to the next one, who whispers it to the next person and so on. The final person then repeats the phrase aloud and it is unlikely to be the same as it was when it started. This effect gets worse as the message passes through more people. If large organisations pass information in informal ways, the Chinese whisper effect is likely to apply and the information may not be passed on correctly.

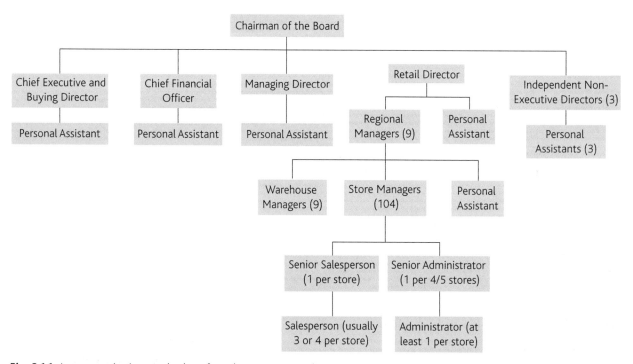

Fig. 3.1.1 *Large organisations tend to have formal management styles*

Did you know?

The most famous example of Chinese Whispers (which may or may not be true) is said to have come in World War I, when a message that started out as 'Send reinforcements, we're going to advance' became 'Send three and fourpence, we're going to a dance'!

It is safest to pass communications on in a written format, to ensure that they get passed on accurately, and formal organisations tend to do this. In the past it would have been done by sending out printed documents through the internal post system following a rigid circulation system, each person receiving the document would initial it and send it on to the next person in the chain, taking a copy for themselves if they needed to. This tends to generate huge amounts of paper as each person copies and files the document 'just in case'. It also takes a long time.

A more modern version of that system would involve e-mailing the document as an attachment to each person on the circulation list or using an intranet to store the document centrally and e-mailing people to tell them that they need to look at it. This is quicker, as everyone can see the document at the same time.

Obviously small organisations need to pass on written communications too, but if a short message needs to be passed on to someone in an office of two or three people, it is probably easier to tell them rather than to send them an e-mail. Shared documents are likely to be stored in a networked folder, rather than needing an intranet.

Whatever the size of the organisation, there will always be an informal communication system going on alongside the formal, official one. Commonly known as 'the grapevine' it consists of gossip, rumours and informal discussion and tends to respond to news much more quickly than any official system can. Any organisation that wants to exert control over the way its information is passed on needs to be extremely careful about its ICT security, setting up strict controls over access rights to documents and building these issues into operational and disciplinary procedures. Taking control by releasing information officially whenever they can will also help, as rumour and gossip tend to thrive most when the real facts are unavailable.

> **Did you know?**
>
> The most common source of leaked information in the House of Commons was once said to be from people leaving an original document under the lid of the photocopier. Or was that just a rumour?
>
> Rumour or not, some newer photocopiers now have a warning sound that beeps if the original is not removed once copying is completed.

End of sub-topic questions

1 Consider your own school or college. Discuss the formal and informal information methods within it, including examples of what information is passed on by each of the methods.

2 For each of the examples given below, state whether they are an example of formal or informal information flow:

- an announcement in school assembly about a change in time for a sports fixture
- a form tutor giving out this year's timetable
- an employee telling another that the boss is being promoted
- the minutes of a production meeting
- an SMS message to a maintenance engineer on standby to come in to repair a server with hard disk failure
- a leaked memo passed to a newspaper reporter.

3.2 ICT strategies and policies

The strategic level managment of any organisation will establish its long-term aims. The ICT **strategy** of that organisation should match those aims and the ICT policies will identify how that strategy will be put into operation.

For example, a seller of specialist food products might have an aim to increase its market share.

Its ICT **strategy** might then include the development of e-commerce.

Its ICT **policy** might include:

- employing a web designer to set up a website with a secure payment system to enable customers to order online and promote the site via search engines and targeted advertising
- a publicity campaign amongst existing customers to encourage them to use the site to send food as gifts setting up an EDI link with a delivery company to make the process as efficient as possible
- setting up arrangements for EFTPOS with the company's bankers.

> **Key terms**
>
> **Strategy:** a long term plan for achieving a goal.
>
> **Policy:** a statement which defines the organisation's position on a particular issue and may determine decisions, actions and other matters.

■ 3.3 The contribution of ICT management to business strategy

If ICT is to contribute effectively to the strategic aims of an organisation, it is vital that it is represented appropriately at strategic management level. The role of the Chief Information Officer is a vital one as they are able to influence organisational strategies. This could involve suggesting areas where ICT can help the organisation to meet its aims or managing the unrealistic expectations of others with regard to what is possible. If the opportunity to have input right at the beginning of the decision process is not available, the ICT system is likely to be a compromise rather than what is ideal because it will not have been given sufficient priority early in the decion-making process.

■ Case study: Chief Information Officers in government posts

The website www.cio.gov.uk is for CIOs in government posts. The CIO Council is the first initiative to bring together CIOs from across all parts of the public sector to address common issues. The work is divided into the following areas:

Transformational Government: the strategy for using IT to transform government and to deliver modern public services more effectively.

Shared Services: how government and the wider public sector can achieve significant savings and increase effectiveness by modernising the provision of corporate services.

Government IT Profession: bringing together IT professionals to create a joined up, government-wide IT profession.

Delivering Success: providing improved leadership to IT-enabled business change programmes and development opportunities to IT professionals in the public sector.

■ Activity

The report at www.cio.gov.uk/transformational_government/strategy/contents gives details of the government's ICT strategy, called 'Transformational Government'.

The webpage www.cio.gov.uk/transformational_government/it_enabled/case_studies/index.asp gives case studies of some government ICT projects.

Read the reports and then write a summary of how the government is using ICT now and how it plans to use it in the future.

■ End of sub-topic questions

3 Explain the difference between an ICT strategy and an ICT policy.

4 Most large organisations have a Chief Information Officer to represent ICT issues at strategic level. Explain why this is important in terms of ICT management.

3.4 Factors influencing ICT strategy

The goals of the business

As was stated at the beginning of this section, the ICT strategy of any business needs to meet its business goals. Any ICT development should provide measurable benefits to its users, to the organisation or to its

Fig. 3.4.1 *Main factors affecting ICT strategy*

clients. A really good development will produce benefits for all three. If the new system is seen by the employees as advancing the business and producing benefits its introduction is likely to be well received and supported. It is well worth taking the time to spell out the benefits to the people involved so that they understand the reason for making changes which in the short term may make their lives more difficult. This applies to users at all levels, including operators and managers who will all have to work with the new system.

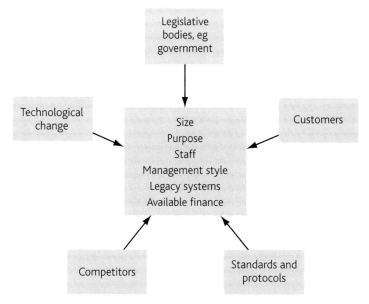

Fig. 3.4.2 *ICT strategies will be affected by many internal and external influences*

Available finance

The financial case for investment in any new system has to be established clearly using cost benefit techniques. These involve calculating the costs of the new system – which may be more complex than would seem to be the case at first. For example: a company is considering combining several smaller systems into one company-wide database accessible from any of its UK offices. Costs might include:

- development of database
- new software licences
- new server hardware
- upgrades to some workstation hardware
- upgrading operating systems to be able to run the new software
- improved communications network to ensure enough bandwidth to deliver acceptable response times
- importing data from legacy systems
- training of users and support staff.

Set against those costs should be improvements in efficiency, a reduction in time spent transferring data between systems, faster response to customer queries, possibly meaning that fewer customer support staff will be necessary. Better response to customers should also attract new clients and keep existing ones who might have moved due to poor service.

A lot of the money would need to be invested up front, whereas some of the benefits may take time to come into being. A financial model would help the organisation decide whether the financial investment is available and, if so, if it would be a worthwhile investment. One way of reducing initial costs might be to consider leasing some of the hardware and software rather than buying it outright. The decision as to whether the investment in a major new system can be justified financially is made at a strategic level.

Legacy systems

The hardware, software and data that make up the existing systems in the organisation need to be considered too. It may not be feasible to replace legacy systems when introducing new ones and the ICT strategy must consider how the old and new systems can work together. This may involve transferring data from the old system to the new one, or ensuring that data portability is considered so that data can be transferred between the systems when necessary.

Geographical factors

The geographical area over which the business operates will also affect its ICT strategies. Communications networks become increasingly important if the company's offices or clients are spread over a wide area. If the entire organisation operates from a small office, a simple LAN will meet its needs, whereas an organisation that is spread over a wide area will need a WAN, perhaps involving leased communication lines. Similarly, if clients tend to live locally to the business, an e-commerce operation may not be justified as they are probably happy to travel short distances. A wider client base is more likely to profit from web-based trading, but good customer support will need to be in place; this must be accessible by methods that do not involve direct contact, i.e. personal visits to the company by the customer. International organisations may have to consider how their security arrangements are affected by legislation in other countries.

Compliance with legislation

Any organisation that stores personal data about living individuals is bound by the terms of the Data Protection Act and the company's ICT strategy must take that into account. This could affect, for instance, whether the company can pass on customers' data to be processed in other countries as part of an **offshoring** arrangement.

Additionally, any employer has a duty of care to its employees regarding their health and safety and the Display Screen Equipment Regulations must be complied with, financial systems must be subject to audit and software use is governed by the Copyright and Patents Act.

Other legislation may apply in particular circumstances and multinational companies may be subject to different legal agreements in other parts of the world.

Key terms

Offshoring: the transfer of an organisational function to another country, regardless of whether the work is outsourced or stays within the same corporation.

Case study: the 'Safe Harbour' agreement

Data protection legislation in the USA is generally much weaker than in Europe. The 'Safe Harbour' agreement was developed to provide legislation that matches European levels, but it is not compulsory for American firms to join the agreement and it is self-regulated. Without appropriate protection, UK firms are not allowed to transfer personal data unless sufficient data protection is in place. The USA tends to have stronger Freedom of Information legislation.

In 2007, the EU and USA reached an agreement regarding Passenger Name Records. These records are generated when a passenger books travel and may contain sensitive data under the terms of the Data Protection Act. PNR allows all the different agents within the air industry (from the travel agent and the computer reservation systems (CRS) to the carrier and the handling agents at the airports) to recognise each passenger and have access to all relevant data related to his/her journey, including departure and return flights, connecting flights (if any), special services required on board the flight, etc.

This data can be passed on to other organisations within the US and may be kept for seven years; furthermore it is not always possible for people to obtain a copy of their records. Many of these terms and conditions would not be allowed under the Data Protection Act and companies working in both the USA and the UK need to be very aware of privacy legislation.

Activity

Do some research on Passenger Name Records and the Safe Harbour Agreement. Do you think that European travellers should be concerned about the use of their data in the USA?

The management of information assets over time

The amount of data collected by organisations has increased in recent years and this trend is likely to continue. Over time, the volume of data that organisations need to store can become extremely large and their information strategy needs to take this into account.

How long data must be stored will depend on the type of data it is. Some financial data, for example, has to be kept for a particular length of time to comply with legislation. The Data Protection Act states that personal data must be kept no longer than is necessary and so such data should be purged regularly. Some data may need to be kept accessible for people to refer to quickly, other data may need to be kept 'just in case' and so can be archived so that it can be accessed, but not immediately.

This volume of data can have an impact on storage methods, backup procedures, hardware and communication systems.

3.5 Corporate ICT strategies

Large organisations need a corporate ICT strategy that applies over the entire organisation if it is to avoid individual departments following their own strategies and, possibly, putting the corporate aims at risk.

Keeping pace with developments

Any ICT strategy needs to consider how it will keep up with technological developments. Future proofing when purchasing new equipment is always a matter of degree, for example, prices for equipment tend to fall rather than rise and so it may not be wise to invest in equipment that is too highly specified, because it is bound to cost more now than it will later. On the other hand, the disruption that is caused by improving or replacing systems should not be underestimated and so a balanced decision needs to be taken at the point of purchase. It is important to consider the ability to upgrade hardware and software in the future and some companies choose to lease rather than buy because upgrades are usually included as part of the leasing process – and it helps to plan budgets.

The frequency with which equipment is to be replaced is an important factor and most companies operate a rolling programme of upgrading or replacement of equipment over a particular time period. Software is similar, in that new software may have better features that will be useful for the company, or it may be important to keep pace with the software clients and competitors will have available.

A corporate strategy will specify how ICT procurement is to take place, how centralised the purchasing policy will be and how much freedom individual departments will have to choose the equipment that they buy.

Information management

Access to information must be defined at corporate level as it is a vital facet of an organisation's operations. The use of a corporate management information system may be desirable, for example, and the corporate strategy would need to take that into account. Issues of security and confidentiality also need to be laid down consistently across the organisation. Security levels and clearances for members of staff need to be carefully thought through to enable decisions about what rights should be allocated to particular network areas and files.

For example, a school might set up the following access levels:

	Head Teacher	Staff	Student
Head Teacher Directory	Full Control	No Access	No Access
Staff Directory	Full Control	Read, write, create	No Access
Departmental Directories	Full Control	Full Control	Read only
Student Directories	Read Only	Read Only	Full Control

This can be achieved by setting up groups of users within the network management software. Rights are allocated to users to control what they can do and permissions are allocated to files and directories to control who can access them and what actions they can perform. A combination of rights and permissions can give very tight control over the organisation's data.

People

The corporate ICT strategy will also consider how the human resources of the ICT staff within the organisation are managed. Recruitment policies may cover the qualifications and experience to be demanded for various types of job, possibly using the BCS structure mentioned in the previous section, to ensure that ICT personnel have the required competencies for the job they are doing. The corporate strategy will ensure that the same rules apply fairly across the company.

Staffing issues also have an impact on security procedures. If data of a particularly sensitive nature is stored, organisations may put in place a system of security vetting for those staff with access to it. Job roles and responsibilities may also be designed in such a way that sensitive job functions cannot be performed by a single employee, but are distributed amongst multiple individuals.

The hierarchy of the organisation and the roles and responsibilities of senior managers will also affect the corporate strategy. Some organisations may centralise the role of the ICT department, while others may distribute ICT staff within departments.

This organisation is structured by function. Each department will be responsible for its own ICT systems, buying applications, equipment or services as they need them.

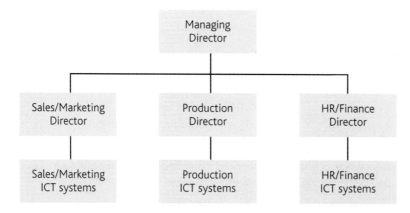

Fig. 3.5.1 *Organisation structured by function*

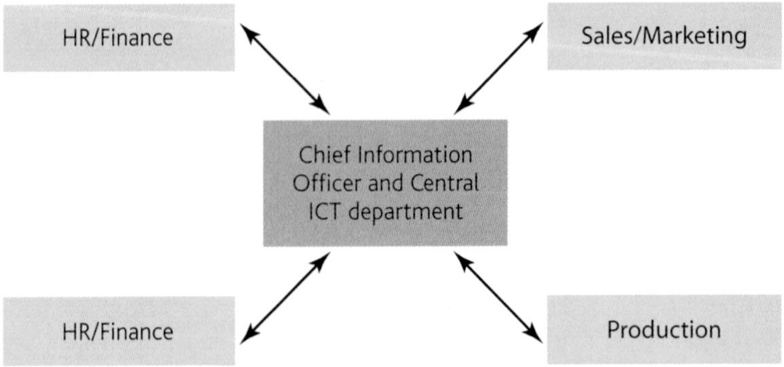

Fig. 3.5.2 *ICT department controlling all information management*

In this organisation, the ICT department controls all information management within the organisation. It defines a centralised strategy for information management and is represented at the highest level of the organisation via a Chief Information Officer.

Standards

Standards and **protocols** apply throughout the ICT industry and must be given consideration when the ICT strategy is established. A communications protocol is an agreed set of rules to ensure the proper transfer of data between devices. If an organisation has decided to adopt EDI wherever possible, for example, procurement policies must allow for this. It may involve initial expense, but should improve the smoothness with which data can be exchanged.

Some examples of protocols are:

Open system is a set of protocols allowing different types of computer to be linked together. These standards are called OSI (Open Systems Interconnection) and are related to other protocols such as TCP/IP (transmission control protocol/Internet protocol).

If a company is offering on-line payment facilities, it must provide secure payment facilities. Most website pages use the http **HyperText Transfer Protocol**, but **https** is a secure version of this protocol with appropriate levels of encryption to protect financial transactions.

File Transfer Protocol (FTP) is the standard used for transferring files over the Internet. When software companies allow users to download patches and updates for their software from their website, they use ftp.

An **IP address** uniquely identifies a physical computer linked to the Internet. The domain name server converts a domain name into its corresponding IP address.

SMTP and POP3 are both e-mail protocols, but POP3 provides more facilities than SMTP.

Key terms

Protocol: a standard set of rules. For example, a communications protocol is a standard set of rules used to ensure the proper transfer of data between devices.

OSI (Open systems interconnection): is a set of protocols allowing computers of different origins to be linked together.

TCP/IP (transmission control protocol/Internet protocol): is the set of working practices that allow Internet users and providers to communicate with each other no matter what type of equipment they are using.

HyperText Transfer Protocol (HTTP): the HyperText Transfer Protocol is the set of rules used on the World Wide Web for communicating between sites.

HTTPS: a secure version of http.

File Transfer Protocol (FTP): the set of rules that govern hardware and software settings when transferring files over the internet.

IP address: uniquely identifies a physical computer linked to the Internet.

Activity

Many organisations publish their ICT strategy online, particularly those in the public sector such as local authorities. Use a web browser to locate a suitable ICT strategy and look for statements that fall under each of the headings listed above.

End of sub-topic questions

5 All organisations using ICT systems will be subject to legislation. Name two pieces of legislation that may apply and discuss the impact they may have on the ICT strategies of an organisation.

6 Explain the term 'future-proofing' as it applies to ICT systems and explain its implications on a company's procurement policy.

☑ *In this section you have covered:*

- the fact that the size of an organisation will affect how formally information flows within it and large organisations are generally more formal

- the need to match the ICT strategy of an organisation to its overall aims

- the importance of the role of Chief Information Officer as a member of the company executive

- the factors that influence an ICT strategy within any organisation

- the need to manage information assets over time, which will involve managing an increasingly large volume of data

- the need to ensure that ICT strategies and policies conform to industry standards.

Policies and legislation

In this section you will cover:

■ policies covering the use of ICT in an organisation

■ the impact of legislation on ICT policies and procedures.

Key terms

Contract of employment: the legal agreement between an employer and an employee.

Disciplinary procedures: lay down the penalties for breaking company policies. These may include verbal and written warnings, fines, suspension and even instant dismissal for cases of gross misconduct.

Security of data: involves making sure that an organisation's data is correct, is kept confidential and is safe.

Privacy of data: involves ensuring that data is not seen or accessed by anyone who is not authorised to view it.

Fig. 4.1.2 *The data on this laptop is not secure because its owner cannot access it, but it is private because neither can anyone else*

4.1 ICT policies

Once an organisation has established its ICT strategy, it must put policies in place to deal with the practical implications of ensuring the strategy is implemented.

Organisations will have policies covering different aspects of the use of ICT, such as security, training and procurement. Many of these policies will form part of an employee's **contract of employment** and breaches of policy will be dealt with in accordance with the **disciplinary procedure**.

Fig. 4.1.1 *Contracts of employment are essential tools in enforcing organisational policies*

Security policy

A security policy is a statement of how an organisation intends to protect its assets. An ICT security policy should aim to ensure the **security** and **privacy of the data** stored on the system to which it applies. In an age where most organisations cannot function without their ICT systems and data, this policy is obviously of vital importance.

An organisation's security policy will initially lay down procedures that employees must follow in order to protect its data and equipment. This includes its hardware, software, data and storage media. It is vital that the security policy is supported by the top levels of management as they are the ones ultimately responsible in law for the organisation's data.

The policy must:

■ identify potential threats to data and manage the risks associated with the threats

■ allocate responsibilities for data security

■ state what resources will be needed to maintain data security.

The organisation needs to analyse its data and establish how valuable it is to the organisation and what the potential consequences of breaches of security might be. These might be financial (e.g. inability to trade), legal (e.g. breaking the Data Protection Act) or to do with a loss of trust from customers or suppliers. It also needs to establish how long the data needs to be kept.

Once the data has been classified it can be allocated a security level and the people who need access to it can be established, for example data might be classified as:

- public – data that can be made available to anyone without risk to the organisation
- internal use only – can be used anywhere within the organisation, but should not be released outside it
- confidential – restricted to certain members of the organisation only.

Network security

Network access rights form an important part of this policy, as do the user names, passwords, biometric identities and any other methods used to control log ins and network privileges. They will cover the minimum length of passwords, the formats they can take and how often they must be changed. The workstations any user is permitted to use can be controlled by the network operating system, as can the times that any user can access the network. Machines can be set to log out the user automatically if no action has been performed over a set number of minutes.

Data transfer

The security policy will also control who has access to the Internet and to e-mail and whether a user or workstation can use removable media such as USB sticks. Data may well be encrypted as it is stored or transmitted to other parts of the system. The level of encryption may vary with the sensitivity of the data and with legal requirements, for example, to protect credit card details. Firewalls should be in place to prevent attacks from outside the organisation.

Change control and monitoring

Procedures can be set in such a way that changes cannot be made without review and approval by senior staff. Network operating systems also generate security logs that can help to detect misuse and potential security breaches such as repeated failed attempts to access a particular user account. Systems can be set up to record exactly what any user has done to any data file on the network. Knowing that their actions are closely monitored can discourage employees from behaving unprofessionally. Sensitive job functions may be split up in such a way that no single employee can perform them alone.

Use of laptops

Laptops pose particular threats to security and organisations must address these risks as part of their security policy. Employees must be aware of what they are permitted to do when their laptop is used out of the office, for example its use by other family members may well be forbidden. Data should be backed up and it may need to be encrypted so that it is unintelligible if the laptop is stolen. Common sense rules, such as not leaving a laptop in a parked car should also be spelled out. Virus checkers should be kept up to date and it may be advisable to call laptops in for checking by support staff at regular intervals.

Backup and recovery policies

These are covered more thoroughly in Section 7, but it is an essential part of any organisation's security policy to establish how data is to be backed up and how it can be recovered in the event of a catastrophe.

Training policy

The training policy covers the training of employees at various stages of their career. Induction training should take place for every new employee and this should familiarise them with the fundamental procedures that

Fig. 4.1.3 *User names and passwords are usually the first step in maintaining data security*

Fig. 4.1.4 *A tiny memory stick can have enough capacity to store the data of an entire organisation*

Fig. 4.1.5 *Company laptops are not intended for home use*

■ Remember

Whilst it is clearly important to protect both equipment and data, it is that data that must take the highest priority. Equipment is replaceable, data is not.

Did you know?

The BCS is the professional organisation for the British computer industry and can give advice on training and career progression. Their skills framework can provide a useful tool for organisations to define the skills required for particular jobs and identify gaps that can be addressed via training.

must be followed. It may also include task based training to introduce them to the actual job they need to do.

Continued training is an important aspect of staff development, helping the employees do their current job well and perhaps prepare them for promotion to other positions. Some training may take place on site and some may be delivered by external agencies. Some organisations allow employees time off to do college or university based courses. Implementation of the training policy is often monitored via the organisation's HR management software.

Section 8, Training and supporting users, discusses options for training and support in more detail.

Procurement policy

A procurement policy is designed to control the purchasing of ICT equipment. It may insist that all ICT equipment is purchased centrally by the ICT department or provide a list of approved suppliers that departments may order from. Many organisations are now specifying that the equipment should be as environmentally friendly and energy efficient as possible. Central purchasing may give the organisation the advantage of discounts for buying equipment in bulk and restricting the number of different models also makes support easier as fewer parts need to be kept in stock. The organisation's attitude to laptops needs to be clear. Laptops are convenient and may be essential for users who move around a lot, but they are expensive to buy and maintain and pose increased security risks.

This policy may also cover disposal of unwanted or obsolete equipment, which may involve selling equipment on, giving it to charitable organisations or disposing of it responsibly, preferably where it may be at least partially recycled.

Consumables are also expensive and if the procurement policy restricts, for example, the printer models available, fewer types of consumable need to be held in stock and discounts for bulk purchase may be available.

PC activity

Use computer magazines and/or websites to obtain prices of business computers that might be suitable for:

a   A small business wishing to use a computer for payroll, Internet access and office support activities such as word processing and simple spreadsheets.

b   A large graphic design business requiring 20 workstations that will be capable of video editing and high level graphics.

You should include:

- operating system software
- office support software
- specialist software such as payroll, graphics and video editing packages.

Remember to look at the software specification to give you an idea of what hardware specification will be needed.

For each business choose two machines, one with the minimum specification and one with a better specification to allow for future-proofing. Set up a spreadsheet that will compare the machines. Explain what extra functionality you would get for the extra money spent on the more expensive machines.

Are there significant cost savings per copy if you buy 20 copies of a software package rather than one?

⬑ Acceptable use policy

An acceptable use policy gives guidance to users about the way they should use the facilities provided by the organisation. It covers such issues as personal use of company e-mail and Internet. Some organisations ban the use of personal e-mail and web browsing entirely, others allow it in rest periods such as lunchtime. All organisations will have rules that prohibit the sending of abusive or defamatory e-mails, and most will reserve the right to read any e-mail sent via its system.

Web access is also covered and this policy should lay down the organisation's stance on the type of content that is not permitted. This may cover obscene or offensive content, but may also restrict the downloading of streaming media such as live video, as this can have a significant impact on the performance of the network. Similarly, downloading files may be forbidden because of the danger of viruses or illegal software. Filtering software can be used to control what sites are accessible and monitoring software is available that tracks all Internet activity against each user name. This may reduce the instances of abuse by acting as a deterrent, but needs to be backed up by disciplinary procedures.

> **▮ Remember**
>
> Company-based e-mail should not be considered private. It should be considered as a postcard that anyone can read rather than a sealed letter.

> **▮ Activity**
>
> A large college has 200 staff and many thousands of students, aged 16 and upwards, many of whom study part-time. All students have login rights on the college intranet and a college e-mail address that they can use to submit assignments. All college workstations have Internet access with a filtering system available. The filtering system can produce reports of exactly what sites each student has accessed and sites can be categorised, e.g. as gambling, games, social networking, chat, etc.
>
> Discuss the categories of website that you feel ought to be completely banned. Should there be any difference between sites available to staff and students? Is it fair that the college keeps records of all Internet sites accessed and failed attempts to access banned sites?
>
> Once you have made your decisions, design an acceptable use policy for the college.

> **▮ Did you know?**
>
> Some organisations have found that when they investigated their network traffic, almost 40 per cent of network resources were taken up by social networking sites.

> **▮ End of sub-topic questions**
>
> **1** For any organisation with which you are familiar, identify:
> **a** an example of data they would make publicly available
> **b** an example of data they would make available to all employees
> **c** an example of data that would have its access restricted to certain employees within the organisation
> **d** discuss how the organisation's security policy can help the organisation enforce these restrictions.
>
> **2** Discuss the threats that laptop use poses to an organisation's data and suggest appropriate security procedures that should be in place concerning their use.
>
> **3** Discuss the statement: 'All the people who work in my organisation are adults, so I don't see why we need an acceptable use policy!'

4.2 The impact of legislation on ICT policies

The AS specification covered the details of the legislation that affects ICT use in organisations. The A2 specification is concerned with the affect that those pieces of legislation have on the practical operations of the organisation via its ICT policies.

Imagine you were appointed as an ICT manager for an organisation and govern the responsibility for that organisation's compliance with legislation. The basic approach for each piece of legislation would need to be as follows:

- make sure you are fully aware of the implications of the legislation for your organisation
- check the current situation to check how well the organisation complies at present
- identify any areas of non-compliance and correct them
- update procedures to make sure the organisation continues to comply
- train staff regarding their responsibilities under the act
- build the procedures into induction training, contracts of employment and disciplinary procedures
- check from time to time that procedures are being followed.

If an organisation does not put appropriate procedures into place to ensure that legislation is complied with then it can be prosecuted as an organisation or individual employees may face prosecution if they have failed to meet their responsibilities.

Data Protection Act

Appoint a data controller who is responsible for the company's data.

Check that the organisation has registered with the Information Commissioner's office and that the terms of their registration match what they actually do with the data.

Look at each of the data protection principles in turn and put procedures in place that identify what needs to be done and who needs to do it. This covers practical details such as:

- The handling of customer requests to view their data – who handles such requests, how are they logged, who checks that response times are adequate?
- Security of data – what access does each employee need, who sets up network rights to control access, who destroys unwanted hard copy?
- How will the organisation ensure that data is updated regularly and deleted when it is no longer necessary?
- Staff must understand that they must not gossip about personal data to which they have access and that if they fail to carry out their responsibilities under the act they will be subject to disciplinary action.

Freedom of Information Act

Public sector organisations are subject to the Freedom of Information Act and if the act does apply to an organisation they must deal with information requests promptly and effectively. The most important implication is to identify what information they must release under the act and what information may be covered by exemptions.

Remember

Security is all in the detail – who changes the backup tapes, who destroys unwanted printout, who checks the backup files can be recovered?

They then need to set up a procedure to handle information requests and collect any payments they deem necessary.

If the information requested would cost a great deal to collect, the person who requested it can be asked to narrow down the information they require.

Computer Misuse Act

Complying with the Computer Misuse Act is largely a matter of staff training and network security.

Staff must understand that their user names and passwords control their rights on the network and that any attempt to access data outside those network rights is a breach of the act and will be subject to disciplinary procedures.

That also means that staff must understand the importance of not sharing passwords or writing them down where they might be accessible to others, not leaving workstations logged in and generally following security procedures.

Access rights on the network must be considered carefully and security features such as automatic logout if workstations are not being used should be employed wherever possible.

Copyright, Designs and Patents Act

The main thrust of this legislation for most organisations will be the control of software licenses.

- Software tools are available that can audit the software that is installed on all workstations across the network. This list then needs to be checked against the list of software licences held by the organisation and any unauthorised software identified.

- Any unauthorised software must be removed or the correct licences purchased.

- Steps must be taken to ensure unauthorised software cannot be installed. This could involve disabling drives that read removable media, banning Internet downloads and restricting permissions to install executable files.

- Staff must understand the importance of only using authorised software and not installing software licensed for company machines on home computers unless the software licence permits it. Again, disciplinary procedures should be invoked on staff breaking this rule.

- The network audit should be repeated at regular intervals.

Some organisations might need to consider the wider implications of this legislation, particularly those involved in producing printed or electronic publications where intellectual property is involved. The content of all this material must be original or copyright free unless permission is obtained from the copyright holder. Stock images are available online that must be paid for but can be legally used in published works and this may be more economical than obtaining images from scratch. Similar libraries of sound files and fonts are also available.

Health and Safety at Work Act

The Display Screen Regulations are the part of the Health and Safety of Work Act that applies to computer users. In fact, it specifically applies

Did you know?

Under the Freedom of Information Act some of the more bizarre requests for information have been for:

- 'an old Royal Navy recipe for sauteed kidneys and curried meatballs'

- 'the weight of the (then) deputy prime minister, John Prescott'

- 'a list of eligible bachelors within Hampshire constabulary between the ages of 35 and 49 and details of their e-mail addresses, salary and pension values'.

None of the requests were able to be fulfilled.

Remember

The main risks from continued computer use are:

- back pain and spinal damage
- eye strain and headaches
- upper limb disorder (often called repetitive strain injury)
- stress.

Did you know?

The website www.webpagesthatsuck. com is one that discusses user interfaces for websites in the hope that considering bad practice will lead to better designs.

The website www.masternewmedia. org/news/2005/04/17/bad_user_ interface_design_can.htm discusses the dangers of poor interface design on a system designed to help doctors prescribe medication and suggests patient health could be at risk.

AQA Examiner's tip

The only part of the Health and Safety at Work Act that directly influences the ICT policy of the organisation is the Display Screen Regulations. Answers about wiring, not taking food and drink near a computer or any other issue that applies to many other types of equipment will not gain marks in the examination.

to workers who use computers for the major part of their working day. Occasional users are not covered, although it is clearly good practice to bear in mind the needs of all employees.

Employers must:

- Carry out risk assessments on all workstations to identify any health and safety issues. Check lists are available that cover all the major issues. The workstation needs to be assessed in conjunction with the user. A setup that is suitable for a very tall person may not be suitable for someone who is much shorter.
- Supply suitable adjustable furniture that means the employee can achieve an appropriate posture with the back well supported, eyes level with the top of the monitor and feet placed comfortably.
- If the office operates a hot desking policy, it is particularly important that the workstation components are adjustable.
- Train users to adopt a safe keying position so that their wrists and fingers are less prone to damage.
- Provide sufficient desk space so that the user can work without adopting an awkward position.
- Consider the tasks the users are carrying out and try to build in changes of activity to reduce the time they spend sitting in one position.
- Provide software that has been designed to good health and safety principles, avoiding garish colour schemes, reducing key strokes by features such as drop-down lists and utilising good menu design with short cuts for experienced users.
- Provide a system through which employees can report health and safety issues and ensure that problems are dealt with rapidly.
- Review workstations at regular intervals.

Activity

Choose one of the pieces of legislation shown above and produce some training material to inform employees of the purpose of the legislation and their duties under it.

End of sub-topic questions

4   Discuss the implications of legislation on the organisational procedures of a business operating an e-commerce site selling software for designing and making greetings cards via downloads or on CD-ROM. You should include:

- The Data Protection Act
- Copyrights and Patents Legislation and
- The Health and Safety at Work Act.

✓ *In this section you have covered:*

- security policies
- training policies
- procurement policies.

The impact of on organisational policies of legislation such as the following Acts:

- Data Protection
- Freedom of Information
- Computer Misuse
- Copyright, Designs and Patents
- Health and Safety at Work.

5 Developing ICT solutions

> **Did you know?**
>
> No-one is certain of the real cost of failed software projects, but in the US alone it is estimated to be upwards of $75bn a year in re-work costs and abandoned systems (www.computerweekly. com/Articles/2007/12/31/230115/ calculating-the-cost-of-failed-software-projects.htm).

Whenever an individual or organisation embarks on a new project, they naturally hope it will be successful, yet a large proportion of new projects fail. ICT projects are no exception to that rule. Indeed, there have been many examples of high profile projects, many of them government funded, that are deemed to have been failures, or at least only partially successful. Examples, according to the Public Accounts Committee, include:

■ Department for Work and Pensions

£149.4m, including £135m costs for the cancelled Benefits Processing Replacement Programme.

■ Department for Environment, Food and Rural Affairs

£26.2m spent on cancelled projects, including the £12.6m Catalyst electronic records system.

■ Department for Transport

£9.2m spent on cancelled projects, including £7.9m on the DVLA's Tracking Vehicles Through the Trade system.

This section identifies some of the factors that should contribute to the development of successful ICT solutions as well as looking at some of the reasons that may cause them to fail. However, before any new project or system development, a feasibility study must be carried out to establish that the development is worthwhile and likely to succeed.

5.1 System development life cycle

ICT systems, whether large or small, have to be developed in stages. These stages can be illustrated in a Systems Development Life Cycle. An

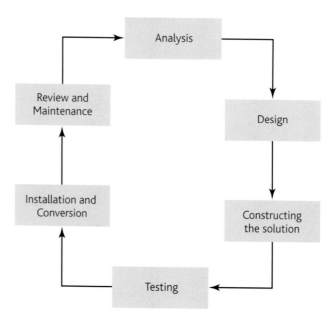

Fig. 5.1.1 *System development life cycle*

important point to note is the use of the word cycle – once started, there is no end to the development of a system. Successful ICT solutions pay attention to each stage of the development life cycle, as failures at any of those stages may cause the entire solution to fail. The most common version of a systems life cycle is shown in Fig. 5.1.2, but in practice it would be a mistake to assume that each of these stages finishes tidily and moves on to the next.

In real life there will be overlap and feedback and designs may need to be amended if unexpected difficulties arise when constructing the solution, thus requiring test plans to be changed and so on. This leads to a slightly different viewpoint, often called the 'waterfall' model.

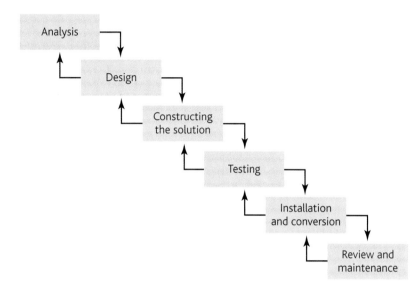

Fig 5.1.2 *System development life cycle (waterfall model)*

At the end of each stage of the life cycle there will be agreed **deliverables** – things that have to be produced and each stage should be signed off by the client together with **approval to proceed** to the next stage.

Stages of development

Analysis

A new system is usually developed to meet a need or solve a problem and it is clearly important to establish the exact nature of that need or problem before a solution can be attempted. Systems analysis is an extremely demanding and important job within the ICT industry and good systems analysts can earn extremely high salaries, because their work forms the foundation of the rest of the development process.

Key terms

Deliverables: documents or systems that must be produced during the various stages of the systems life cycle.

Approval to proceed: a signed agreement from the client that they are happy for the next stage of the life cycle to commence.

Activity

Revise the personal qualities required for ICT professionals from Section 11 of *AQA Information and Communication Technology AS*. Which of the qualities do you think would be most important for systems analysts? Look online or in magazines for advertisements for systems analyst posts. Do they agree with your findings?

■ **Remember**

The client is the person who needs the solution to a problem and the user is the person who will actually use the solution. The audience is the person or persons at whom the final product is aimed. For example, a company may commission a new website. The client is the company, the users are the people who keep the content updated and the people who view the site on the web are the audience. Not all ICT developments will have an audience.

The first step in the process of developing a new solution is to analyse the system that is currently in place. This may be a manual, paper-based system or an existing computer-based system that is no longer adequate or, for example, one of several systems that need to be combined into a single more efficient one.

The analysis needs to establish:

■ exactly what the existing system does

■ what its strengths and weaknesses are

■ what is required of the new system

■ any constraints that may be placed on the new solution, for example by legal requirements.

Section 6 of *AQA Information and Communication Technology AS* covered analysis – and may well be worth revisiting at this point. It emphasised the need to develop a clear list of client/user requirements to ensure that the ultimate solution meets their needs.

The main methods by which the analysis is carried out were also covered in Section 6 of *AQA Information and Communication Technology AS*, but in summary they are:

■ interviews with users, at all levels of the organisation, who will have requirements of the new system

■ questionnaires and surveys to record opinions

■ analysis of existing paperwork

■ observation of users of the current system.

This helps to identify key processes and operations and weak areas in the current system.

The analysis would make use of formal data analysis techniques such as:

■ identifying processes via data decomposition diagrams

■ mapping processes to **data flow diagrams**

■ showing detailed input/process/output via **system flow charts**.

Deliverables at this stage could include:

■ **Key terms**

Data decomposition diagram: a diagram that represents the processes within a system.

Data flow diagram: a diagram that shows how data moves through a system, showing where the data comes from, what processes it passes though and where it goes to within the organisation.

Systems flow chart: a diagram used to define the flow of data through a system.

■ clear and detailed user requirements specification (signed off by the end user to show that they have agreed it)

■ a list of tasks and subtasks that need to be completed, together with a schedule of timings

■ a Gantt chart, or critical path analysis that can be used as a basis for project management

■ an assessment of the users' current ICT skill level and training requirements

■ hardware and software requirements and limitations

■ performance indicators or evaluation criteria, matching the client/user requirements, which will be used to measure the success or failure of the project.

■ an outline of the proposed method of solution.

■ **Remember**

A requirements specification could include data capture, system function, user interface, output, storage and security requirements.

Design

Whereas the analysis describes **what** the project is going to do, the design explains, in detail, **how** it is going to do it.

It will include detailed descriptions of:

▦ the software, tools and techniques to be used, together with a justification as to why they have been chosen

▦ data capture and validation methods

▦ designs for the user interface

▦ processing to be carried out

▦ outputs to be produced

▦ how the solution is to be tested.

Deliverables:

▦ details of file definitions, data structures and processes

▦ designs of outputs, whether on screen, on paper, or by other methods

▦ a test strategy and plan, including test data to be used for module/ unit testing, integration testing, systems testing, user testing and operational testing

▦ a detailed time plan for this stage of the project.

Again, these designs should be approved by the client before construction commences.

Constructing the solution

There are two main ways of constructing ICT solutions.

Customising a package

If a generic or special purpose package exists that is suitable to be used for producing the solution, it is probably the cheapest and quickest method. Special purpose packages may just need to be configured to meet the needs of the organisation, but generic packages will probably demand a greater degree of customisation. Solutions built on standard packages may require compromises as the designer will not have the completely free hand that building a bespoke solution from scratch would give. However, solutions built this way are probably less risky than those coded from scratch and more help and advice is likely to be available from other users, developers' forums or, if necessary, consultants. Of course, customising a package may still involve writing modules of code to make the solution perform efficiently for the client.

Writing code

Writing code gives the designer much more flexibility to produce a solution that fits the client's needs exactly. It is likely to take longer than customising an existing package and there is a considerably increased likelihood of errors that will need to be picked up by testing. For genuinely innovative solutions there is always a higher probability that a practical working solution may not be found and the degree of risk of creating a custom solution should have been established at the analysis stage.

Whichever way the solution is constructed, it is vital that it is documented as it is being built. A draft user guide will also need to be produced so that it can be tested during the testing procedure.

Deliverables:

▦ working system

▦ documentation of solution

▦ draft version of user guide.

◤ Testing

It is vital that any new system is thoroughly tested before it goes live. Testing involves working step-by-step through the test plan, with the test data produced in the design stage and recording the results of the tests. Any tests that do not produce the required results will be the subject of corrective action.

Module/unit testing

Module testing is sometimes known as unit or component testing and it involves testing the individual sections of the software to make sure that each section works as intended. They tend to be written from a programmer's perspective. Module testing is an example of **white box testing,** where the tester has access to the internal data structures and algorithms that form the basis of the system.

Integration testing

When module testing is completed, the modules are combined one at a time at each integration stage and **debugged**.

Functional testing

Functional testing is intended to test the operation of the system and may pick up errors that were missed at the module/unit testing stage. They are the first indication that the solution is likely to meet its user requirements specification and tend to be written from a user's perspective. Developers write functional tests with users and then test the system exhaustively with variations on those tests. Functional testing is an example of **black box testing**, where the system is judged on whether a given input produces the correct output, rather than concentrating on exactly what is happening inside the system.

Systems testing

Systems testing tests the complete, integrated solution in preparation for user testing. It checks that all the modules operate together properly and that a transaction is processed correctly throughout the system from beginning to end.

User testing

User testing is where the actual users of the system will put it through its paces and offer their comments. It is the final stage of testing before the system goes into operation and should result in acceptance by the client that the system can be installed. This can be a crucial stage, as users may do things in ways that the system developer had not envisaged. For this reason, testing the user documentation is an important part of this stage.

Operational testing

Operational testing is conducted in the actual environment in which the solution will be working, or perhaps a simulated version of that environment. Using a simulated environment gives the testers more control over the conditions the solution experiences, and tests can be repeated, but it is only a partial substitute for seeing the system under real operational loads. Which approach is adopted will depend on the system itself and the type of installation that is envisaged.

Deliverables:

- test data and results
- modified user guide
- client approval to install.

Key terms

White box testing: checks the details of the processing code and algorithms.

Black box testing: checks that a given input produces the correct output, rather than the details of the processing involved.

Debugging: the process of testing program code to isolate and remove errors.

Did you know?

A failure to test software thoroughly was blamed for the problems that caused chaos on the opening day of Heathrow's terminal 5 in 2008. The baggage handling system could not cope with the load upon it and failed to recognise a number of bags. The fact that the building of the airport ran over and reduced the available time for testing may have been one factor, and it was obviously not possible to test the system under live conditions until the terminal was open. The amount of bags in practice greatly exceeded the number that had been placed on it in test modelling.

Remember

Section 7, Introducing large scale systems, will consider testing, installing and maintaining large scale ICT systems in more depth.

Installation and conversion

This is the crucial stage of development that sees the system put into its working environment to be used by the client. It also involves conversion of any existing systems that will be superseded by the new solution and linking to any other systems with which it needs to operate.

The system documentation will be presented to the client at this stage, including the operational user guide and technical documentation that may be needed for future maintenance.

Most of the training of users will now need to take place, although some training may have gone on in advance based on a simulated environment. The developers are likely to remain on site until they are happy that the new solution is fully functional and operating correctly before the solution is handed over to the client.

Deliverables:

- fully functional solution, signed off by the client
- full documentation including user guide and technical documentation.

Review and maintenance

Once the system is installed and operational it must be carefully monitored. This monitoring is not something that simply takes place for a few days or weeks, it is a continuous, ongoing process. The system is constantly reviewed to ensure that it is providing the functionality required by the organisation. As a result of this monitoring, maintenance of the solution will take place. There are three types of maintenance that the system is likely to undergo:

Corrective maintenance

Even after undergoing the most rigorous testing possible it is likely that there will still be errors in the system. **Corrective maintenance** involves putting right any reported errors once the system has become operational.

Adaptive maintenance

It is inevitable that the way in which an organisation operates will change over time. **Adaptive maintenance** is altering the system to meet the new requirements of the organisation. It may also be necessary to respond to changes outside the organisation such as new legislation or security threats.

Perfective maintenance

Perfective maintenance is where any inefficiencies that have been identified as a result of reviewing the system, are investigated and the system 'tweaked' to make it as efficient as possible. It may also involve adding extra functions to make the solution even better.

Inevitably over a period of time the new solution will be overtaken by new developments in technology or major changes in the needs of the organisation to the point where it is no longer viable to continue to use it. At this point, the life cycle will go back to the analysis stage and a new solution will replace it.

Key terms

Corrective maintenance: involves putting right any errors that remain in the system after testing.

Adaptive maintenance: involves making alterations to respond to changes in the organisation or external changes such as a new security risk.

Perfective maintenance involves: improving the software to enhance its performance.

End of sub-topic questions

1 Even when an ICT system has been thoroughly tested, maintenance may still be required.

Explain, giving examples, three different types of maintenance and why they may be necessary.

5.2 Successful ICT development

Factors that may aid a development's success

There is no sure-fire guarantee that any development will be successful, but there are certain factors that make it more likely:

Management and end user involvement

The development process is much more likely to succeed if the staff, at all levels of the organisation, who are likely to use it are involved at appropriate stages. Different levels of user will have different requirements and it is important that they are all taken into account if the system is to be a success. Involvement in the initial analysis ensures that the requirements specification allows for all of the users, not just some. It is easy for one person to assume that they know what someone else needs, but it is much better to ask that person directly. Operational level users often have far more knowledge than they are given credit for and can make extremely valuable contributions.

Similarly, the same range of users needs to be involved in testing the system and its user documentation. The users also need to be trained properly so that they begin their work on the new system with a confident and positive attitude.

Realistic expectations

It is important that the management expectations are realistic and that they are not expecting the system to do the impossible. A clear specification should ensure that all parties realise what the solution will be aiming to achieve. The time frame and budget also need to be realistic in order to allow sufficient time for the system to be tested thoroughly before installation. Managers may need some initial training in ICT in order to achieve this.

Professional standards

The development team need to have high professional standards. They need to have the appropriate skills to do what they are doing well and the appropriate attitude to want to produce the best product they can, avoiding the temptation to 'cut corners' on parts of the development that may not be particularly visible. The development needs to be documented thoroughly at all stages, so that if one team member falls ill or becomes unavailable for any other reason, a new developer can pick up where they left off. This documentation should follow industry-standard methods.

If the development team is working to high professional standards they will ensure that every stage of the systems development life cycle is completed thoroughly and client approval is sought at every opportunity.

Good teamwork

In some respects, this is linked to professional standards. ICT developments are unlikely to involve just one person and the members of the team must work together to ensure a successful outcome. All members must stick to the project plan and communicate any problems to their team leader immediately so that they can be taken into account in schedules.

Factors that may cause a development to fail

In a similar way, there are certain factors that make it more likely that a newly-introduced system may fail and these factors may occur at any stage in the systems life cycle.

Did you know?

A service level agreement may help to ensure that expectations are realistic. It is a document that defines, as far as possible in measurable terms, the standard of service the client can expect. For example, it might state that customer support must be available 24 hours per day on weekdays only, a response time for 90 per cent queries must be one minute or less and that weekly reports must be available by 9am on Mondays.

Inadequate analysis

If the analysis is not done thoroughly, it is likely to miss details that may turn out to be extremely important. It is the analyst's job to bring any issues that may cause problems to the attention of the client, as the client does not necessarily have enough knowledge to spot them. The implications of each of the requirements needs to be explained in language the client is likely to understand, so that when a client signs off a requirements specification he or she understands what is to be developed.

Poor design

If the design does not take into account all factors of the analysis fully, the solution is unlikely to be successful. Poorly-chosen techniques may make the system slower than it needs to be and inappropriate interfaces can cause frustration for users. Poor design may also make a system less robust than it should be, and a system that crashes or freezes is unlikely to be popular either.

Inappropriate testing

If the test plan is inadequate or the test data is badly chosen, major errors in the solution may go undetected until the system is installed. This is also likely to be a problem if testing is not allocated sufficient time, which sometimes happens if other areas of the development have been allowed to over-run in terms of time or budget.

Poorly organised installation and changeover

If the installation of the new solution does not go smoothly it will affect the attitude of the users and that is not an easy situation to retrieve, even if the situation is later rectified. If staff training has been inadequate, the system will get off to a bad start and any mistakes made may affect the output, perhaps leading to a lack of client confidence.

Poor user support and maintenance

It is unlikely that any new development will go entirely without a hitch, but if the support and maintenance team are on hand and can deal with problems effectively, issues can be picked up and dealt with quickly. If users are left to fend for themselves, they are likely to develop a poor attitude to the solution, which will adversely affect its chances of success.

Poor project management

The next section deals with project management in more detail, but the most likely factor that could lead to a failed development is if the project plan goes out of control. If problems start to occur they can usually be dealt with if they are reported early and dealt with efficiently, with the critical path through the project being updated appropriately. This may involve reallocation of personnel to tasks that are likely to overrun so that the timings remain as close to schedule as possible. If this does not happen, there is a danger that some other part of the systems development life cycle will be skipped, to the detriment of the final product. There is a similar danger if costs overrun and money runs out before testing can be completed properly.

■ **End of sub-topic questions**

2 Explain three factors that are likely to make a newly-developed ICT project successful.

3 'The reason this project failed was nobody asked us what we wanted' is a comment sometimes made by users of ICT systems. Discuss the role of analysis in the development of ICT systems, including the people who should be involved at this stage.

■ 5.3 Formal project management

Given the importance of project management, it is vital that the task is managed systematically and the use of formal methods is likely to be the best way to achieve this.

Project management involves breaking down a large task into smaller ones and for each of those allocating an appropriate amount of time at an appropriate point in the schedule. Resources such as people, equipment and budget also need to be built into the plan to ensure that correct resources are available when the project demands them. Specialist staff will almost certainly be working on other projects and be booked for a limited period of time. For example, if on week 23 of a schedule a new piece of software is to be tested in a simulated operational environment, it will need personnel with appropriate testing skills plus access to the computer suite in which the testing will take place. This may have to be booked with a specialist company well in advance. If project schedules are allowed to overrun, the staff may be tied up with other projects and the suite providing the simulated environment may not be available. For this reason it is essential to monitor progress carefully and react quickly and efficiently to any situation that may cause the project to fall behind.

Projects need to have:

■ a defined timescale

■ an approved budget

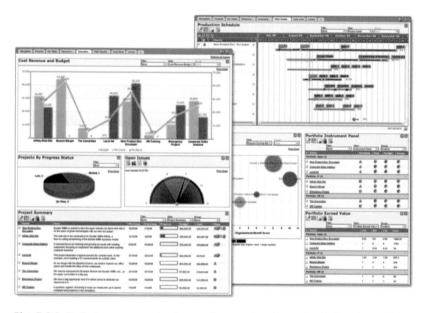

Fig. 5.3.1 *Project management software allows project data to be displayed as useful information*

limited resources – an agreed amount of labour and equipment.

Project management is made up of:

- a set of specialist skills, knowledge and experience to reduce the risks and improve the likelihood the project will succeed
- a suite of tools such as document templates and registers, planning and modelling software, audit checklists and review forms (see Figure 5.3.1)
- techniques and processes to monitor and control time, cost, quality, risk and issue management.

Project planning

Various plans need to be drawn up:

Project Plan	Outlines the activities, task dependencies and time frames
Resource Plan	Lists the human resources (skills, roles, responsibilities) and equipment resources (specifications, quantities) needed
Financial Plan	Allocates financial budget to each stage of the project
Quality Plan	Lists clear quality requirements for each deliverable and outlines how these will be met
Risk Plan	Documents foreseeable risks, what can be done to reduce the likelihood of the risk happening and how it will be dealt with if it does
Acceptance Plan	Criteria for client acceptance, and schedule for client acceptance reviews
Communications Plan	How everyone involved will be kept informed of progress – what method will be used and how frequent progress reports will be
Procurement Plan	Goods and services to be obtained externally and the process by which suppliers will be chosen

	11.03	12.03	1.04	2.04	3.04	4.04	5.04	6.04
Preparation and planning								
Develop project proposal	■							
Approve project proposal		◆						
Recruit project team		■						
Development and test								
Specify detail requirements			■					
Develop prototype				■				
Approve prototype					◆			
Develop beta verson					■			
Test beta version						■		
Apply final corrections								
Approve final version							◆	
Implemantation								
Train users							■	
Roll-out final version								◆

Fig. 5.3.2 *A Gantt chart is a useful visual technique for documenting project schedules*

Planning a schedule is not as simple as listing one task after another. In some cases two tasks can be carried out by different members of the team at the same time and at some points the work will not be able to move on to the next phase until the previous one has been completed. For example test data can be gathered whilst the solution is still being designed, but testing cannot begin until that data and its accompanying test plan is available. Critical path analysis is a technique that examines the task list and the accompanying schedule and works out which tasks take longest and which are dependent on earlier tasks having been completed. From this, the critical path can be established – the shortest possible time in which the project can be completed and which tasks that path depends upon. If those critical tasks run over schedule, the whole project will be delayed. If less critical tasks run over, it may not be as important, and so the project manager may be able to shift extra resources to the critical task to avoid an overall delay. Most large ICT projects will have penalty clauses that mean that if the project is not delivered on time the development company will be paid less, so keeping to schedule is vital for all concerned.

An article at www.gamedev.net/reference/articles/article1440.asp explains the critical path analysis for a computer game developer.

Remember

De facto standards are standards that have developed because a lot of people have adopted them.

Case study: PRINCE

PRINCE® (PRojects IN Controlled Environments) is a project management method that was originally developed for the UK government and is now widely recognised as a de facto standard for project management. The latest version of the PRINCE method is PRINCE2.

PRINCE2 is a simple to follow project management method that can be tailored to suit a variety of projects. It covers how to organise, manage and control projects to ensure they are completed on time and within budget. It helps the project manager manage risk and control quality and change.

PRINCE2 is a process approach to project management, fitting each process into a framework of essential components which need to be applied throughout the project. It sets out to:

- work out what roles should be involved in the project, what they will be responsible for and when they are likely to be needed
- use processes and controls to give the project structure and define what information should be gathered as the project progresses
- divide the project into manageable chunks or stages, allowing more realistic forward planning and control of resources
- provide a common language between customers, users and suppliers, bringing these parties together on the Project Board. This should reduce the number of mistakes, saving time and effort.

PRINCE2 has been developed to be compatible with other techniques such as SSADM.

Project management software

Project management software is a useful tool to set up and monitor project schedules, budget and resource allocations. It can be used to plan:

- agreed deliverables for each stage of the project so that both client and development team know what has to be produced
- milestones – these are critical stages in the development of the project where progress can be assessed to ensure that the demands of quality, time and budget are all being met
- client sign off at the end of each stage and approval to proceed before commencing the next stage.

Project management software allows a project to be broken down into sections, each of which can be planned and then linked to the other sections to produce an overall plan.

As progress is made, the initial project plan is updated with what actually happened, such as how long things took and how much they cost. The software allows the effect of any changes that may occur to be modelled to show the overall impact on the project schedule and budget. It allows the user to draw charts, like the ones mentioned above, to produce reports on various aspects of the project, such as budgets, and to use the data generated by the project to generate information to help them make decisions about how well the project is going and what needs to be done next.

End of sub-topic questions

4 Discuss, giving an example, the importance of formal methods when planning and developing an ICT project.

5 Explain three features of project management software that make it a useful tool for managers of ICT based projects.

5.4 Development methodologies

Development methodologies tend to fall into two categories, linear methodologies such as the waterfall method and iterative methodologies such as Rapid Application Development.

Linear methodologies are sometimes called heavy methodologies and are generally developed from methodologies used in engineering. In recent years, agile methodologies have become popular for some developments as they tend to be more adaptable to changing requirements, although they are generally not considered suitable for large scale system development.

Case study: BT

In 2005, telephone company BT began replacing their aging phone-traffic monitoring system. The new system has made the work of phone-traffic controllers much easier. The entire system was completed in 90 days using an agile development cycle. Prior to the move to agile development, it could take three to nine months for a third-party developer to gather specifications. Then the development itself could take up to 18 months or longer to complete.

Source: www.infoworld.com

Linear

The waterfall model outlined earlier is an example of a linear methodology, where each stage of the process begins when the previous one has been completed. There will be a certain amount of 'splash back' – revisiting an earlier stage because of an unforeseen difficulty – but on the whole the phases will take place in sequence.

This style of methodology tends to be easier to manage than iterative ones and close control over time schedules and budgets is possible. It does tend to be inflexible, however, and less able to respond creatively to problems and opportunities that present themselves along the way.

Iterative

Iteration is a process of repeating a sequence of steps until the required answer is achieved. Iterative methodologies loop round the stages of the development until the developers and/or the client are happy with the solution at that point and can move on to the next stage.

Prototyping

Prototyping can be used as a development methodology that relies on a process of continuous refinement based on experiences at each stage. Small stages of the solution are built and refined, with as much user involvement as possible, so that the prototype gradually evolves to meet the user's requirement. Because the user is heavily involved with the development, there is an increased probability that they will be happy with the finished product.

For many designers, prototyping feels like a more natural way to work, allowing a gradual process of idea and refinement to create the best solution, but there is a danger that the overall focus of the work becomes lost in the details and that time and budget become less easy to control.

Agile methodologies

There is currently a lot of debate in the ICT industry concerning the use of the waterfall method versus agile methodologies. Agile development methodologies claim to be a great deal more adaptable than more traditional methodologies.

The waterfall method is a defined methodology. That means that the development team plans first and then enforces those plans. Agile methodologies involve first producing brief, high level plans and then adapting and extending those plans based on the results of what actually happens. They involve breaking down the development into small pieces (e.g. design, coding and testing sections) and fitting the pieces together at an appropriate time.

Examples of agile methodologies include:

Extreme Programming (XP)

The XP methodology is based on user stories written by the clients as things that the system needs to do for them. They are in the format of about three sentences of text written by the client in their own terminology. Acceptance tests are then created to verify the user story has been correctly implemented.

User stories differ from traditional requirements specifications in their level of detail. They only provide enough detail to estimate how long the 'story' will take to implement. When the time comes to implement the

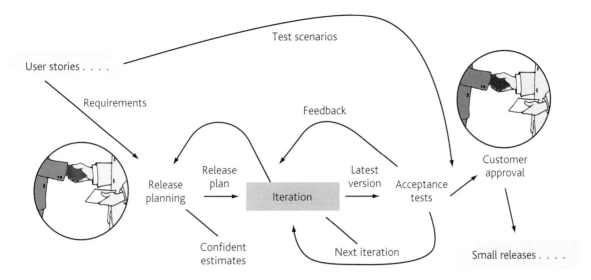

Fig. 5.4.1 *Extreme programming*

story developers will go to the customer and receive a detailed description of the requirements face to face. This allows changes in requirements to be included more easily than in traditional methodologies.

A release planning meeting is held for clients, developers and managers to create a schedule that everyone agrees on. An iteration planning meeting is then held to establish what is to be done in the first iteration, probably of about three weeks in length. Automated tests are used as far as possible to speed up the development and the solution is gradually refined using a series of iterations.

See www.extremeprogramming.org for more information.

Scrum

The name Scrum is taken from the scrum formation in rugby where, as in scrum development, people fulfilling distinct tasks come together to form an effective whole. Scrum divides a problem into a set of discrete tasks assigned to groups. It relies on short meetings designed to address immediate problems and keep tabs on progress on a frequent basis.

> ### Did you know?
>
> You can get more information on Scrum by going to www.computerweekly.com/Articles/2007/09/04/226507/applying-scrum-and-other-agile-development-techniques.htm.

Fig. 5.4.2 *The name Scrum comes from the name of the formation in rugby*

Crystal

There are several versions of the crystal methodology, but they are all based on the premise of centring the focus on people and teams rather than processes. Crystal methods seek to find the simplest and most compact team structure and process for an organisation, thus making the development process faster and more efficient by reducing paperwork and bureaucracy and improving communication.

Rapid Application Development (RAD)

RAD uses computerised development tools, along with prototyping, to improve development times and quality at relatively low financial costs. It uses such tools as:

■ Graphical User Interface (GUI) builders
■ Computer Aided Software Engineering (CASE) tools
■ Database Management Systems (DBMS)
■ fourth Generation Programming Languages
■ code generators
■ object-oriented techniques.

The emphasis in this method is on meeting the business need quickly, and at an acceptable cost, rather than creating the most technically perfect solution.

RAD proposes that products can be developed faster and of higher quality by:

■ using workshops or focus groups to gather requirements
■ prototyping and user testing of designs
■ re-using software components
■ following a schedule that defers design improvements to the next product version
■ keeping review meetings and other team communication informal.

Dynamic Systems Development (DSDM)

DSDM is really an extension of RAD, based on the following principles:

■ user involvement produces accurate decisions – the key in running an efficient and effective project
■ the project team must be empowered to make decisions that are important to the progress of the project without waiting for higher-level approval
■ a focus on frequent delivery of products allowing testing and review so that improvements can be made at the next iteration or phase
■ the main criteria for a deliverable is delivering a system that addresses the current critical business needs rather than a perfect system
■ development is iterative and driven by users' feedback
■ testing is carried out throughout the project life cycle
■ communication and cooperation must be efficient and effective.

End of sub-topic questions

6 Give a brief explanation of the difference between linear and iterative methodologies and suggest factors that might influence which methodology might be chosen for a particular ICT project.

✓ *In this section you have covered:*

Factors that contribute to successful ICT system development, including:

- management and end user involvement
- realistic expectations
- professional standards.

Factors that may contribute to the failure of newly- introduced systems, including:

- inadequate analysis
- poor design
- inappropriate testing
- poorly organised installation and changeover
- poor user support and maintenance
- poor project management.

The systems development life cycle and stages of development:

- analysis
- design
- construction of solution
- testing
- installation
- maintenance.

Development methodologies, including:

- linear methodologies such as the waterfall methodology
- iterative methodologies and prototyping
- agile methodologies such as extreme programming, scrum and crystal.

6 Systems development tools and techniques

- techniques for investigating and recording systems and processes
- the use of data modelling tools
- techniques for testing systems.

Activity

Create a mindmap which identifies guidelines for interviewing.

6.1 Investigating and recording techniques

Students need to be aware of the techniques available and their appropriate uses.

Interviews

One-to-one interviews are perhaps the most usual method of gathering client requirements and are usually considered to be the most productive. An open-ended discussion may be useful to get the interviewee talking and then more probing questions can be asked to establish the requirements in more detail.

Group interviews work well when there are several people at similar levels who need to be involved. They require careful preparation to avoid losing focus, but the discussion of ideas and opinions can be very valuable in establishing a full set of requirements. To be successful, interviews must be prepared carefully in advance, conducted smoothly and recorded adequately. A formal report should be prepared as soon as possible after the interview.

Joint Application Development (JAD)

In Joint Application Development sessions a group of people get together and stay in session until a complete set of requirements is documented and agreed to. The client and the users can be involved in regular JAD sessions and the fact that they are so heavily involved is thought by many people to lead to faster development times and greater client satisfaction. It tends to be particularly successful in projects where a number of different users are involved, especially if their responsibilities do not fall into traditional departments or specialisms. The benefit of this approach is that everyone discussing the requirements together means that they have to come to a joint agreement about what is required.

The website www.umsl.edu/~sauterv/analysis/488_f01_papers/rottman.htm gives more information.

Questionnaires

Questionnaires are probably most useful for users in remote locations or for people whose role is going to be fairly minor but who may still want to be involved in the process. Additionally, they can be used to great effect when large numbers of people are involved, but is it fairly unlikely that they will all agree exactly what is needed, because of their different roles and needs, or due to differing personal preferences. A large number of questionnaires will allow you to judge the weight of opinion behind a request – do most people want a particular function or is it just one or two? Often, to ensure that questionnaires are valid, a random sample will be interviewed to check the responses and investigate in more detail.

Observation

Visiting the company to actually see what happens can be very important. A manager may have explained in an interview how the data backup service works but seeing it happen will make it all much clearer. Users who have been doing the same job for a long time may not be conscious of everything that they do, because it has become second nature to them and they don't think about it. Watching such users work may give a better understanding of everything that goes on, what happens when problems occur and how they are dealt with. It also provides an opportunity to observe informal communication such as telephone calls which may not appear in paperwork but may still be important.

Thought showers

If a very new problem is being tackled, a thought shower session may be useful. This is an open session when everyone is encouraged to submit their thoughts. It gives all the participants a change to share ideas, however unlikely some of them may seem at first. This creative process may sometimes produce truly innovative ideas and solutions.

Record searching/document analysis

Record searching or document analysis, means the study of material written down about the organisation or data that it generates. For example, when investigating the back-up service of a large company, there will probably be a procedure manual that describes the procedures involved. Considering this alongside observation of the process will help to confirm what happens and to highlight errors or problems.

Analysing documents used in a system can also identify the data that needs to be stored, the information that needs to be produced and the format the information needs to take.

> ### ■ Remember
>
> This topic was also covered in Section 6, Analysis and design, in *AQA Information and Communication Technology AS*.

Fact recording

Recording the findings of an investigation is an extremely important because:

- it provides a permanent record
- several people may need to work on the same project and need access to the information
- findings may need to be checked and confirmed with other users and this needs a written record as evidence
- the act of recording the findings provides structure and so helps analysis.

Unstructured findings

These can be facts or opinions given in interviews. A standard discussion record may be used in some organisations.

> ### ■ End of sub-topic questions
>
> **1** A large hospital supports ICT users from a central department. It covers facilities used inside the hospital, but also portable equipment taken to local clinics and the homes of patients by specialist nurses and physiotherapists. The department feels that it could make better use of its support facilities by setting up specialist units rather than routing all issues to whichever support staff happen to be free. This will involve tracking requests more carefully and routing them to the most appropriate unit, who can then respond appropriately.
>
> Discuss techniques you might use to gather information about the current system and the requirements for its replacement, taking into account the various levels of staff you may be dealing with.

■ 6.2 Business process modelling tools

As part of the analysis phase of the development life cycle, it is essential to understand the processes that go on within the organisation and document them in such a way that everyone involved can follow and understand them. The use of diagrams can avoid the need for long descriptions and can make the processes clearer.

There are many software packages commercially available to help analysts define and model business processes using some of the techniques that follow.

Structured Systems Analysis and Design Methodology (SSADM)

SSADM is the standard method for analysis and design of large scale applications for the UK government, and can be used in conjunction with the PRINCE2 project management method mentioned in Section 5. It uses a combination of text and diagrams throughout the whole life cycle of a system design, from the initial design idea to the actual physical design of the application. It is a very precise methodology that divides the development into many small stages. Because of the rigid structure of the methodology, SSADM is praised for its control over projects and its ability to develop better quality systems.

Information flow diagrams

Information flow diagrams are used to show how information moves between the parts of an organisation, both internally and externally. It uses the following symbols:

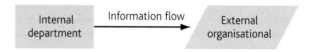

Fig. 6.2.1 *Symbols used in an information flow diagram*

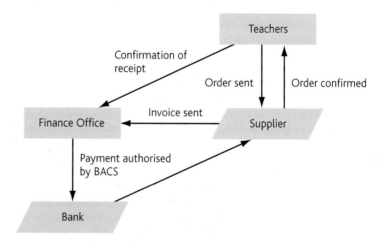

Fig. 6.2.2 *Example of an information flow diagram*

System flowcharts

A system flowchart shows how data and information flows through the system, including manual operations and manipulation of information. A system flowchart should **not** have any decision boxes. The following table shows the most commonly used system flowchart symbols, although there are alternatives.

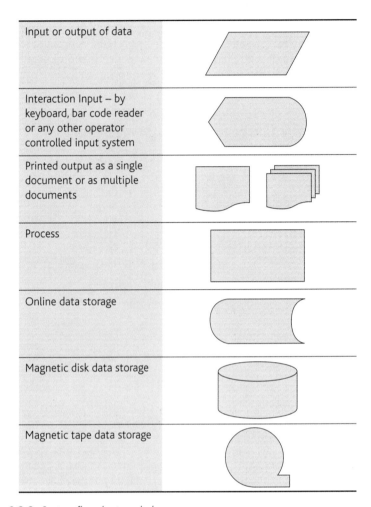

Input or output of data	
Interaction Input – by keyboard, bar code reader or any other operator controlled input system	
Printed output as a single document or as multiple documents	
Process	
Online data storage	
Magnetic disk data storage	
Magnetic tape data storage	

Fig. 6.2.3 *System flowchart symbols*

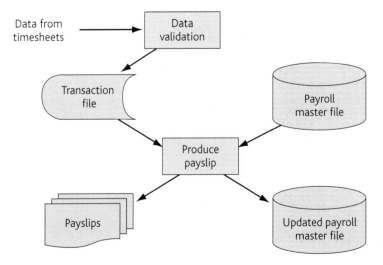

Fig. 6.2.4 *Example of a system flowchart*

Remember

System flowcharts take a physical approach to illustrate the processes that take place in a system. They do not contain decision boxes.

Data flow diagrams show how data moves through a system, identifying where data comes from within the organisation, where it goes to, where it is stored and what processes it goes through on the way. The focus of this type of diagram is the organisation and what it does with the data.

Program flowcharts document what is to happen within a computer program, as opposed to within the organisation. Symbols are used to represent the operations carried out by the computer and flow lines show the sequence of operations. A program flowchart forms part of the permanent record of a finished program and is needed for maintenance purposes, as the person carrying out maintenance may not be the original programmer.

Decision tables

Some business processes involve decisions. It is useful to define the logic behind how a decision is made. Some decisions are simple and can be explained in words, e.g. if the order total is over £50, discount the total by 4 per cent. Some situations may become very complex with large numbers of rules and possible actions. A decision table is designed to help you make sure that all possibilities are considered and to document all the possible outcomes.

Condition	Value of Condition		
Action	Value of action		
Stock below re-order level?	N	Y	Y
Has it been ordered?	N	N	Y
Place an order		X	
Do nothing	X		X

Fig 6.2.5 *Decision table for stock ordering*

Activity

Create a decision table for the following scenario: a college will offer a student a place if their interview is satisfactory, their school reference is OK and they have the right GCSE grades. They will be placed on the waiting list if their school reference is OK and their interview is satisfactory or they have the right GCSE grades. Their application will be rejected if their interview is not satisfactory and they do not have the right GCSE grades.

Data flow diagrams

Data flow diagrams are developed from system diagrams such as the one in Figure 6.2.6. They identify where the data comes from, the processes it passes through and where the data goes to.

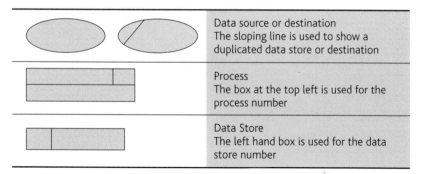

	Data source or destination The sloping line is used to show a duplicated data store or destination
	Process The box at the top left is used for the process number
	Data Store The left hand box is used for the data store number

Fig. 6.2.6 *DFD symbols*

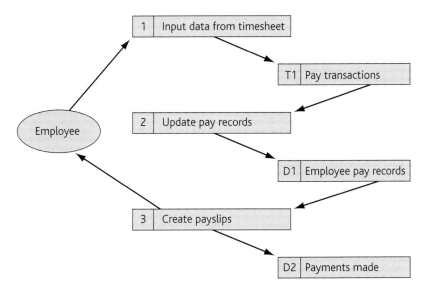

Fig. 6.2.7 *Data flow diagram for the system shown in Fig. 6.2.4*

End of sub-topic questions

2 In the hospital system mentioned above, the user will make a request for support by calling a central number. The operator will take details of the request, create a numbered job record and send it to the appropriate support team who will then respond. The user will be given the job number so that they can track progress if they need to and the support team will update the job record as they deal with the problem.

Create a system flowchart and a DFD for this part of the system.

6.3 Data modelling tools

Entity attribute diagrams

An entity attribute diagram shows the **relationship** between an **entity** and the **attributes** that describe it.

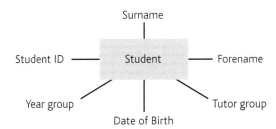

Fig. 6.3.1 *Entity attribute diagram*

Entity relationship diagrams

An entity relationship diagram shows how two or more entities are related.

Symbols used in entity relationship diagrams:

Key terms

Relationship: describes the link between two entities, for example a student and a member of staff might be linked by the relationship 'tutor', which means that member of staff is a tutor to that particular student.

Entity: in databases, the entities are the things that have data stored about them, for example, in a system concerning a school, a student would be an entity.

Attribute: describes an individual data item within the entity, for example, student surname, forename and date of birth.

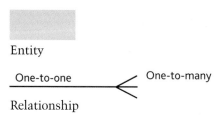

Entity

One-to-one   One-to-many

Relationship

Looking at the example of a student studying subjects in college:

From left to right – one student studies many subjects:

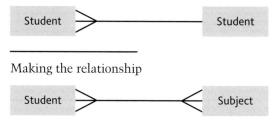

The 'crow's foot' on the end of the line is used to show a one-to-many relationship.

And from right to left – one subject is studied by many students.

Making the relationship

Many one-to-many relationships such as this are difficult to implement in databases and so a new entity of 'Set' is added. One student can have many sets and one subject can have many sets, but one student is in one set for any single subject.

Fig. 6.3.2 *Entity relationship diagrams*

Two one-to-many relationships are more efficient than one many-to-many relationship and make it possible to build an effective relational database.

Activity

If you enter the term 'business modelling tools' into a search engine, you will return hits to many commercial products. Within your group, look at a selection of these products and make a note of the types of diagram and report they can produce. Many of the packages have on-screen demos to show the software features.

Produce an on-screen presentation to demonstrate the results of your research.

End of sub-topic questions

3 A sports centre has many members who book courts and pitches for matches. For this process, draw:
- a systems flow chart and
- a data flow diagram.

4 Identify the entities that are involved in the booking system and draw:
- entity attribute diagrams and
- entity relationship diagrams.

6.4 Techniques for testing

There are a variety of techniques that are used to ensure thorough testing, including:

Test harnesses

Test harnesses allow some types of testing to be automated. A framework is set up that tests units of the programming code under specified conditions and monitors its outputs and processes. This software can launch the tests and analyse the results produced, removing the need for the programmer to do these repetitive tasks and giving them a framework on which to build their testing. This is economical in terms of time and therefore money.

Volume testing

Volume testing is designed to show how the system will perform with different volumes of data. A database may work perfectly well with small volumes of data, but perform badly under heavy loads, giving unacceptable response times or failing to work at all. These tests concentrate solely on the volume of data and set out to establish the useful limits of the software under heavy load, to ensure it meets its specification and can cope with the projected capacity of data that can be expected.

Scalability

Scalablity testing is designed to make sure that the system will function correctly and give acceptable performance levels when the system is scaled up to its full requirements. A series of performance tests are carried out as the system is scaled up, until performance levels start to drop. At this point, data from the test results are analysed, along with other indicators, in order to identify bottlenecks that may be affecting the system's performance.

Prototyping

Prototyping is not strictly speaking a testing method, but it is a useful technique for gathering feedback from clients about the user interface and improving it following their comments, allowing their feedback to be gathered throughout the development process rather than just at the end. In this technique you build a limited version of the solution and show it to the client, who may give additional requirements. You make the required changes and show it to the client again. This process repeats until the solution meets with the client's approval.

Multi-platform

Many ICT systems will need to operate on a variety of **platforms**, rather than assuming all users operate from PCs running a version of Windows. There are software applications available that will automate this process to some extent by running tests on a variety of target platforms. These applications link up to the software provider's system in order for the tests to be run. This could include Apple machines running MAC OS or business machines running Linux. Increasingly, users are looking for

Key terms

Platform: a combination of hardware and software, in particular operating systems software that allows applications software to run.

applications that can also run on mobile devices and this may need to be taken into consideration too.

◨ Use of simulated environments

It may not be feasible to test the system in every environment it could possibly meet and so simulated environments can be extremely useful in testing how they might perform. For instance, if software needs to operate over a client's WAN, it is difficult and time consuming to install and test it in that environment. It is also difficult to control the exact conditions that the software might meet, as load on the WAN may be unpredictable. The use of a simulated environment means that test conditions can be repeated over and over again to test various configurations as fair comparisons.

Did you know?

The BCS have a range of qualifications for software testers. More information can be found at www.bcs.org/server. php?show=nav.6942

End of sub-topic questions

5 Explain why it is that, even if a new piece of software has been fully and correctly tested, errors may still be found when the software is released for general use.

Activity

The website www.testinggeek.com/video.asp gives a set of videos discussing testing issues. Play them through to improve your background knowledge of testing.

☑ *In this section you have covered:*

Investigating and recording techniques, including:

- interviews
- joint application development (JAD)
- questionnaires
- observation
- mind showers
- document recording.

Tools for modelling business processes and data, including:

- system flow charts
- data flow diagrams
- entity attribute and entity relationship diagrams.

Techniques for testing, including:

- test harnesses
- volume testing
- scalability
- multi-platform
- simulated environments.

Introducing large scale systems

In this section you will cover:

- the effect of scale on the introduction of an ICT system
- the challenges posed when testing large systems
- the installation of large systems
- backup and recovery strategies
- maintaining large scale systems.

Introducing large scale systems brings in extra complications and difficulties that may not be present in a small system, posing such questions as:

- How can the reliability of large ICT systems be ensured by testing?
- How can a successful installation be carried out for large ICT systems?
- What strategies are needed for backup and restoration?

7.1 Scale

Large ICT systems can be used not only within a single organisation but also across multiple small organisations For example, ordering systems used in newsagents or NHS systems used across the country in trusts but also in a single GP surgery.

Did you know?

Many Britons on holiday abroad still like to buy their English newspapers and many of the daily papers send the content of each issue to printers abroad so that the customers get their news much more quickly than they used to when papers had to be flown out from England.

Case study: ICT systems used in newspaper production

Newspaper distribution is an extremely time-critical business – a day old newspaper has no value – and so newspapers need to be printed, distributed and sold in just a few hours every day. Journalists produce copy for the paper in different areas such as news, sport and politics. Some of them will be working remotely and will submit their copy to the office electronically. The content of the articles will pass to sub editors who will make the content fit into the space available and the advertising department contributes articles, layouts and illustrations for the adverts that contribute heavily to the running costs of the paper. When submitting advertisements, some customers will send in finished artwork that the newspaper simply needs to insert, other customers will rely on the designers at the newspaper to turn their raw material into a finished advertisement. Editors will oversee the layout, which is then passed electronically to the printers who actually print the papers. All of these users are relying on different kinds of ICT system that must communicate with each other effectively.

Other systems have to be able to transfer data accurately between suppliers, who sell the raw materials such as paper and ink and the printers. The newspapers are sent to wholesalers who sell and distribute them to the individual newsagents, or to chains of newsagents who sell the papers. The shops can order quantities of papers and magazines using EDI.

In addition, very few newsagents sell only newspapers and magazines, so they are almost certainly interacting with suppliers of other goods and services, and this will usually involve other ICT systems.

i Case study: WHSmith

Ordering system

In June 2006 WHSmith News began piloting electronic ordering systems to reduce its paper flow and cut costs.

The newspaper and magazine wholesale arm of the high-street retailer, at that time, distributed more than 50 million newspapers and magazines each week and handled 120 million pieces of paper a year in its supply chain. Information systems director, Richard Webb, said that parts of the supply chain had been in place for more than 200 years. 'All our deliveries to retailers involve paper processes, from invoices to remittance processing and returns,' he said. 'We saw an opportunity to replace some of those processes to cut costs.'

WHSmith News had previously begun a pilot scheme delivering advance details and credit acknowledgement to its own branches and to Tesco.

'The next step is to implement it for all retailers and then provide electronic invoice and remittance,' said Webb.

This trial was part of an IT project to streamline processes and reduce operating costs but WHSmith News was also completing the implementation of warehouse management software from SAP to improve sales-based replenishment.

Improved warehouse management processes had already reduced the number of unsold magazines and newspapers by 20 per cent, saving £1m a year.

However, Gartner Research Vice President, Andy Kyte, said that the biggest challenge facing WHSmith News was its diverse customer base, ranging from major IT-enabled retailers such as Tesco and Sainsbury's to smaller business such as corner shops. To address this, paper and electronic ordering processes were run in tandem until those that were ready to become IT-enabled had made the transfer. In time, smaller businesses are likely to adopt the electronic system and so the paper-based system will cease to be necessary.

This dilemma is typical of those facing large scale system upgrades in that it forces a decision about what to do with legacy systems. Replacing older systems entirely is likely to be the most efficient solution, but is also likely to be expensive. The compromise solution of running two systems is clearly not ideal, but if the alternative is to tell smaller customers they can no longer be supplied, then neither is that. Sometimes such issues force difficult decisions. In this case, for example, it may cease to become financially viable to continue with the paper-based system if very few customers use it.

Case study: NHS systems

The NHS provides the majority of healthcare in the UK, from general practitioners to hospitals, long-term healthcare, dentistry and ophthalmology. Established in 1948, the NHS undertook to provide a free health service, including hospitals, family doctors and public health facilities. It is administered by the Department of Health.

General practitioners (GPs) have registered patients for whom they are responsible. They refer patients, when necessary, to specialist consultants in hospitals. Health visitors, midwives and district nurses provide further services, often in patients' own homes.

Many NHS trusts had their own ICT systems and, within their area, individual GP surgeries would also have their own ICT systems. Other health-related services, such as social care, would also have their own systems. System compatibility between all of these different organisations was a major problem and so an ambitious plan was developed to produce a national information system. NHS Connecting for Health came into being in April 2005, aiming to help the NHS to deliver better and safer care to patients, via new ICT systems that link GPs and community services to hospitals.

The website www.connectingforhealth.nhs.uk gives details of the latest status of the project.

There is no doubt that the new scheme has come under a lot of criticism from many quarters.

One of the initiatives of Connecting for Health was the creation of the NHS Number which provided a unique identifier for each patient that could be used right across the NHS rather than a different one for each doctor, hospital or service used, but even this apparently simple step has not proved easy to implement in all areas of the NHS. Difficulties with contractors, a lack of agreement about exactly what the system needs to provide and patient worries about privacy of their data are just a few of the issues that have caused difficulties for what is undoubtedly one of the largest ICT systems ever implemented in this country. Many people still feel the system is necessary and will deliver huge benefits, saving time and money. You should read the conflicting reports for yourself and make your own decision.

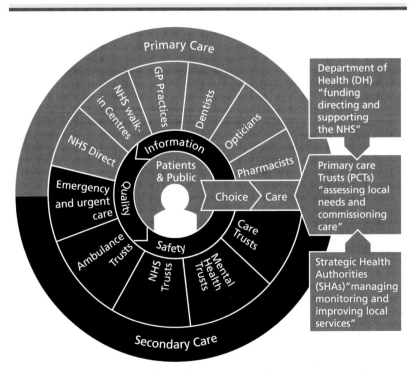

Fig. 7.1.1 *The NHS Connecting for Health scheme aims to improve communication between the many agencies involved in delivering health care*

What both of these systems have in common is the requirement to connect many organisations of varying sizes, which need to transfer data quickly and efficiently across wide geographical areas. The scale of these systems, and the variety of people using, them makes them demanding to install and maintain and their reliability is of great importance to the people who depend on them.

Activity

Read the latest information on the NHS project from the website mentioned above. Then perform an Internet search for articles offering opinions on the new NHS scheme. Record these websites in a table with the following headings:

- name of website
- URL
- date of article
- information given by website
- likelihood of bias.

Based on the evidence you can find, do you think that the implementation of such a large scheme is a good thing or a waste of money? Justify your opinion, making sure you check your facts from more than one source if possible.

End of sub-topic questions

1 Using an example other than the ones listed above, discuss the following question: 'What effect does scale have on the development of ICT systems?'

7.2 Reliability and testing

Testing large ICT systems is a complex task, but it is essential to ensure that the systems operate reliably.

Ensuring that large ICT systems always operate as expected

The functionality of the ICT system needs to be thoroughly tested to ensure that it will operate as expected. The test engineers will be looking for defects under the following categories:

- Functional defects, for example if a decision support system does not produce the quality of information expected of it. This could be because the rules for the decision were not specified correctly or the algorithms used in the code did not fully match the rules.
- Performance defects, for example if a search produces the required result but does so at a speed that is not acceptable. An example might be a knowledge based system supporting a call centre offering technical support, where speed of response is crucial to the number of clients that can be handled per day.
- Usability defects, for example if the users find the interface is inefficient and slows down data entry, perhaps because menu options are illogical for the most commonly performed operations, or expert users are forced to use the same interface as novices and so are slowed down.
- Security defects, for example if a user can accidentally damage the system because warning and confirmation screens are inadequate, or encryption is not high enough in level.

Designing testing to ensure reliable operation

As mentioned in Section 5, an important part of the systems development life cycle is testing the software to ensure it operates reliably. It is sometimes said that the purpose of testing is to make the system fail. Certainly, it is true to say the purpose of testing is to expose the system's weaknesses so that they can be corrected. The earlier the testing commences in the development lifecycle, the better. The test plan will be established at the design stage, together with data sets that will test the software with normal, extreme and erroneous data. Considering budget, schedule and performance in test plans increases the likelihood that testing does take place and is effective and efficient. Planning also ensures tests are not forgotten or repeated unless necessary for regression testing.

Requirements-based testing

The requirements section of the specification sets benchmarks and provides the basis for testing the software. Ideally the test team should be involved in the writing of the specification. They should help to ensure:

- that all requirements are clearly written and not ambiguous
- that all requirements are capable of being tested.

The test team should be developing test cases as the specification is being developed and this forces the team to look critically at the specification.

The test plan outlines the entire testing process and includes the individual **test cases**. A test plan should cover the program systematically to ensure that testing is thorough, but not unnecessarily repetitive, a testing process that does not depend upon accidental, random testing.

Program testing

While program testing is important, it can never guarantee that the code is completely error free, and is usually carried out by applying test cases to the code. It can also be carried out by inspection, where a small team will read through the code during a group meeting, analysing it against a checklist of common problems which the team will be looking for. Walkthrough is a similar technique, where the team manually executes the code using input from test cases. Debugging programs provide facilities to help programmers investigate the conditions where errors occur.

System testing

This makes sure that the system works according to the specification and is done by following the test plan to test that individual system functions work with normal and extreme data and that the whole system produces the correct results for the data input.

Regression testing

As the system is developed, it is likely that changes will be made in response to tests that have been carried out. Regression testing involves re-running earlier tests against the modified code to establish if the changes have created problems with features that worked previously and writing new tests if necessary. It is important to keep a look out for side effects – fixing one problem may create another one.

Change control

Change control is a process designed to make sure that changes happen in a controlled and coordinated way and are properly documented. When a change is proposed, it is important to assess the possible impact of the change on all the parties involved.

> ### Key terms
>
> **Test case:** a set of test data and its expected outcomes.

> ### AQA Examiner's tip
>
> Program and regression testing techniques tend to be used for coded solutions and therefore are less likely to apply to your INFO4 project.

Alpha testing

Alpha testing is carried out by the software house while the software is being developed, based on the test plan and data established in the design phase. The full process of unit, module and system testing will take place using typical, extreme and erroneous data to identify problems and errors. Users may have some input into alpha testing. The results of these alpha tests may sometimes require modifications to the design or implementation of the software so that gradually the software becomes reliable enough to be tested with a wider range of users.

Beta testing

Beta testing involves the software being tested by a selected group of real users who use the software under their normal operating conditions. The users report back any difficulties they encounter and the software can be modified before it is released fully.

If the software is being specifically written for a particular organisation, then this form of beta testing is not appropriate, so a modified form of it, known as 'User Acceptance Testing' is used. This may happen initially on a pilot basis for just a few users so that any errors or problems can be corrected.

Techniques such as test harnesses, volume testing, scalability and the use of a simulated environment (see Section 5, page 44–59), will be built into the test plan and used to test the system at appropriate points in its development. The testing will involve staff from the development company as well as users at all levels, who should be involved at all stages, but particularly in end-user acceptance testing.

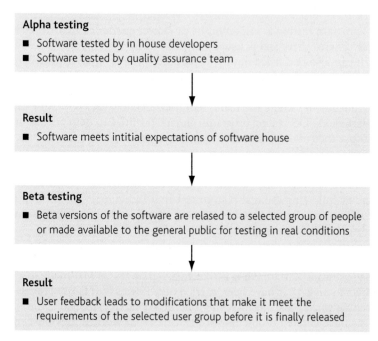

Fig. 7.2.1 *Stages of testing*

Testing network-based systems

As large organisations will inevitably be operating over a network, it is essential that software is tested in a networked environment. User rights and file permissions and storage of common files, such as library files, need to be carefully thought through and tested to ensure that the software functions as expected and response times are acceptable. Simulated network environments may be used to test this functionality.

WANs tend to have less spare capacity than LANS, and have less available bandwidth, carrying large amounts of data over great distances, so any surges in load are likely to have a greater effect on performance. The testing of network-based systems requires specialist skills and facilities, particularly if the network is a WAN. WAN emulation/network simulation technology behaves like a real WAN or wireless environment. It allows testers to recreate a wide variety of different WAN or wireless conditions, ensuring that software can be tested at every stage of its development. These conditions can be replicated as often as they need to be during testing. An example can be found at www.itrinegy.com.

End of sub-topic questions

2 A new ICT system was thoroughly tested at the software house before it was installed. When it was tested on site the users found that it did not work properly over the LAN.

- Give reasons why network based systems are more difficult to test reliably than those running on standalone computers.
- Explain the role of simulated testing environments in overcoming this difficulty.

Did you know?

Network commands that can be used to diagnose network problems include:

Ping: a computer network tool used to test whether a particular host is reachable across an IP network. It is also used to self test the network interface card of the computer. It works by sending ICMP 'echo request' packets to the target host and listening for ICMP 'echo response' replies. Ping estimates the round-trip time, generally in milliseconds, records any packet loss and prints a statistical summary when finished.

Trace route: shows the series of successive systems a packet goes through en route to its destination on a network.

7.3 Installation

This section works through the essential considerations that need to be a part of a successful installation plan for a large-scale ICT system.

Methods of introducing systems

When a new ICT system has been created and thoroughly tested, it is ready to 'go live'. That is, it is time to start using it in the workplace. There are four different methods of introducing a new ICT system into the workplace, which are:

- direct changeover
- phased changeover
- pilot running
- parallel running.

Direct changeover

With a direct changeover the old system stops and the new system is started up. This normally happens after a break of some kind. For example, the organisation may close down for a two week holiday period and, during these two weeks, the new system is installed, so when staff return from holiday they start using the new system.

Advantages

- the quickest of all of the methods (as long as it works)
- less risk of staff being confused between the old system and the new system.

Disadvantages

- difficult to train staff as the new system is not available beforehand for people to train on

- can be more stressful for users as they may not have been trained, and, the old system is gone, so there is nothing to fall back on if there are problems with the new system
- very stressful for the system developers, as they have a very small window to get the system installed and transfer data and files from the old system
- most risky of all the methods, as if the new system does not work for any reason, the old system is no longer there to be used.

Pilot running

Pilot running involves the new system replacing the old one, but only on a small scale, such as in a single branch of the company or in one location. If the pilot works correctly then it is gradually 'rolled out' over the rest of the company.

Advantages

- much easier to control as the pilot can be halted at any time
- easy to monitor and evaluate because the new system can be compared with the old system which is still running in other parts of the company
- easy to train staff by using the pilot system as a training system
- low risk, as if a small scale pilot fails then not too much has been lost.

Disadvantages

- it is usually very slow to roll out a pilot to completely replace the old system
- a pilot may not show problems that exist in a full-scale system. This is because some problems only surface when the system is working under full capacity with larger volumes of traffic
- the organisation will for a time be running on two different systems.

Phased changeover

In a phased changeover the new system is brought in stages (or phases), each stage replacing a part of the existing system, if a phase is successful then the next stage is brought in, until eventually the new system fully replaces the old one.

Advantages

- a very structured method allowing each phase to be fully evaluated before moving on to the next one
- less risky than a direct changeover
- staff can be trained by being taught the new skills required on each phase as it is introduced.

Disadvantages

- slower than direct changeover
- although each phase can be evaluated easily, the complete system cannot be evaluated until all stages have been completed
- integrating each phase with the existing system can be complex and cause complications.

Parallel running

Parallel running involves the old system and the new system running alongside each other, but working independently. The performance of both systems is compared and if the new system works as planned it gradually takes over.

Advantages

- the systems can easily be compared to check if the new system is delivering the expected improvements
- if there are any problems with the new system, the old one can still be used, so this method has the lowest risk
- staff can be trained gradually on the new system.

Disadvantages

- this is a very expensive method as both systems are being run as fully operating versions, so both are doing the same work; this may mean duplication of some staff and hardware
- staff may be confused by having to remember and use two different sets of procedures.

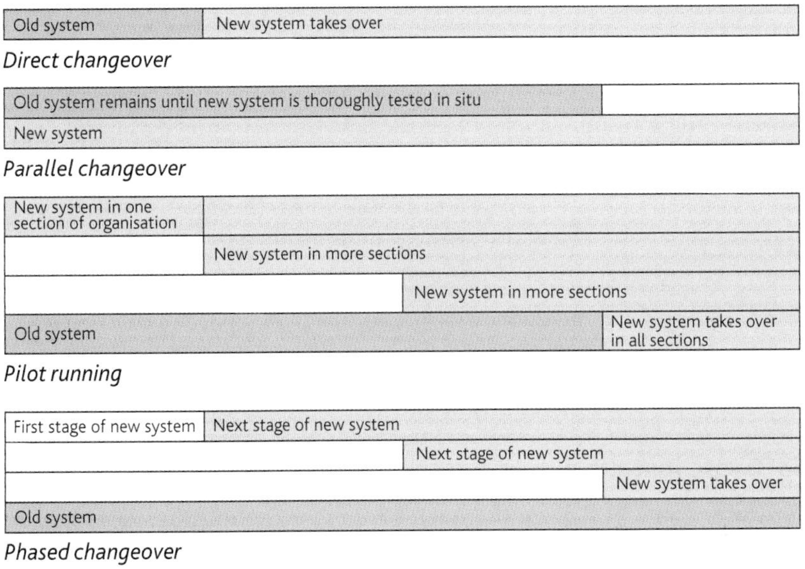

Old system	New system takes over

Direct changeover

Old system remains until new system is thoroughly tested in situ	
New system	

Parallel changeover

New system in one section of organisation			
	New system in more sections		
		New system in more sections	
Old system			New system takes over in all sections

Pilot running

First stage of new system	Next stage of new system		
		Next stage of new system	
			New system takes over
Old system			

Phased changeover

Fig. 7.3.1 *Changeover methods*

Hardware installation and testing

There is much more to the installation of hardware for an ICT system than might at first be thought. For this reason it is essential to have a detailed plan. Usually a designated planning project manager will be responsible for producing a documented plan, which should include:

- a list of responsibilities and the person assigned to them
- a schedule for the activities to be performed – this helps to ensure that hardware is delivered at the right time. For example, there is no point in having a large number of workstations arrive to be set up before the network or power cabling is in place
- a diagram of the proposed (or new) system showing hardware location, content and configuration details, including network cabling, power cabling, hardware specifications and layout of computer rooms and workstations. Consideration also needs to be given to equipment and furniture installations, which must allow sufficient clearance space for safe working
- hardware specification sheets providing detailed information of hardware, including dimensions, electrical, power, temperature, environment and service requirements

■ **Remember**

Modern server hardware will generally need to be installed in an air-conditioned room and this type of installation work will need to be completed before the computer equipment is installed.

■ **Remember**

Cabling runs are usually installed using plastic trunking to protect them from damage.

Fig. 7.3.2 *Labelled cabling in a switch cabinet*

- each major activity phase, such as installation of network cables, bridges, routers, etc., will need to be tested and the results of those tests will need to be documented
- a plan for communicating appropriate elements of the plan with key personnel (for example, seller, installer, management).

Cabling

If the new system involves the need for network cabling to be installed or replaced, it will need to be carefully designed and planned, often by a specialist installer who has the qualifications, tools and testing equipment necessary to ensure the installation meets industry standards. Cabling needs to be carefully documented and labelled to make the tracing of faults easier. Cable routes need to be considered carefully to make sure the runs are as economical as possible, do not exceed maximum lengths, do not expose the cable to physical damage and do not run too closely to electrical power lines because of the risk of electrical interference.

Installation of power cabling needs to ensure that there are sufficient power sockets in suitable places for the equipment that is needed and servers will, additionally, need uninterruptible power supplies and possibly backup generators in case of power failure.

■ **PC activity**

Using CAD software, produce a design for a computer room based on one of the rooms in your school or college. You may use Internet-based software from www.bhg.com/decorating/arrange-a-room or www.ikea.com.

Software installation and testing

Software should have been thoroughly tested by the software development team before it is installed on site. However, despite the most rigorous testing it is still possible that there could be teething problems during installation and operation. The software developer and the computer technicians will need to work together with the end user to ensure that the software is installed and operating successfully. The following tasks are involved in software installation:

- identifying which items of hardware must be operational and available. For example, the system may need the server and some workstations operating, but remaining workstations may be installed later
- ensuring that all manuals applicable to the installation are available when needed
- installing the software
- checking installed software for accessibility by different levels of user
- initializing databases and other software with appropriate data
- conversion from the current system, possibly involving running in parallel
- dry running of the procedures in operator and user manuals
- initializing user-specific data
- setting up queries and other user inputs
- performing sample processing
- generating sample reports
- planning and conducting training activities

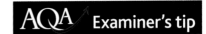

- providing user support and technical assistance for the installation
- conversion from the current system.

Documentation

The creation of the system should be accompanied by appropriate, detailed documentation throughout its development. This documentation should be produced to professional standards and should include program flowcharts, results of testing, technical manuals and user guides.

AQA Examiner's tip

In INFO4 you will be expected to develop your own ICT solution. You will need to make sure the documentation to your solution meets these criteria too.

Resources

Resources can include buildings, hardware, software, infrastructures, finance and people. A major consideration of a successful installation in an organisation is to carefully examine which of its resources will:

- be required for the installation
- be utilised by the new system
- no longer be required
- need to be improved.

For example, a large organisation could have the necessary technical expertise among its own staff to carry out the entire installation; alternatively, they may have to consider buying in support from an external service provider.

Training and support are important resources for any new system, and are a significant factor in creating positive attitudes amongst end users. Section 8 covers methods of supplying user training and support in more detail. Training may need to be started long before the installation of the new system in order for staff to be ready when the system goes live. Extra support will be required as the new system settles in, before dropping to a more normal level.

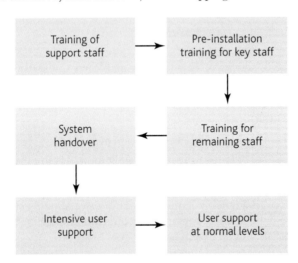

Fig 7.3.3 *Training and support for new development*

End of sub-topic questions

3 Discuss the relative benefits and limitations of the different methods of changeover when introducing a new ICT system into a large organisation.

4 When installing a new information system in a large organisation a detailed installation plan is needed. Describe three of the factors that should be considered when devising an installation plan, justifying why each is important.

ⓘ 7.4 Backup and recovery

Having made the huge financial investment that is inevitably involved in commissioning a large-scale system, it is obviously essential that the data remains secure and available for use. Section 14 of *AQA Information and Communication Technology AS* discussed backup in some detail, and so the focus in this section is on large-scale systems and their specific requirements.

The most useful way of approaching the decisions about backup and recovery is to put in place a **disaster recovery strategy**.

■ Key terms

Disaster recovery strategy: makes plans to avoid data loss and reinstate a working system within an acceptable period of time.

Risk analysis: used to identify each element of a successful information system and to place a value to the business on that element. It then identifies any potential threats to that element, predicting the likelihood of the threat occurring, calculating an overall risk figure, and indicating a degree of severity.

Recovery time objective: the length of time that it will take to get a system fully operational after a crisis.

Data recovery point: the last point at which data can be recovered, i.e. the time lapse between backups.

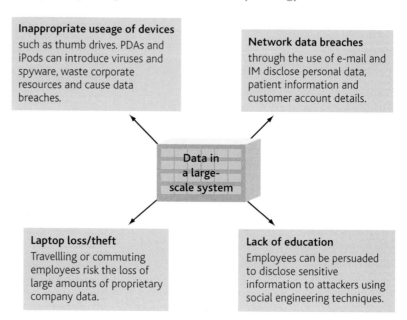

Inappropriate useage of devices such as thumb drives. PDAs and iPods can introduce viruses and spyware, waste corporate resources and cause data breaches.

Network data breaches through the use of e-mail and IM disclose personal data, patient information and customer account details.

Data in a large-scale system

Laptop loss/theft Travellling or commuting employees risk the loss of large amounts of proprietary company data.

Lack of education Employees can be persuaded to disclose sensitive information to attackers using social engineering techniques.

Fig. 7.4.1 *Risks posed to data by employees*

The first stage in setting up this strategy is to carry out a **risk analysis** that identifies the main types of data in the system and, for each of them, identifying:

- ■ their value to the organisation
- ■ the speed with which they need to be recovered.

For example, most organisations rely heavily on their e-mail system and would find it difficult to function without it. They are also likely to have huge databases containing mission critical data. These applications need to be recovered quickly if any disaster or error should cause their failure. Other data, such as personnel records, are important and must be recovered, but are not so urgent.

For each type of data, the organisation needs to set a **recovery time objective**, or RTO. This defines the maximum time allowed to reload recovered data and get the system fully operational again.

They also need to make a decision about how much data they could afford to lose. This involves establishing a **data recovery point**, which is basically the full time that has elapsed since the data was last backed up. For example, if the data is backed up overnight, the data recovery point is last night and there is the potential to lose 24 hours worth of data.

Reducing the RTO is expensive and so it is important to balance the importance of the data against the potential cost.

This analysis should then help the organisation to develop a backup strategy with backup methods appropriate to each type of data.

In addition, the following resources all need to be available:

- suitable rooms
- computer systems
- communication networks
- personnel.

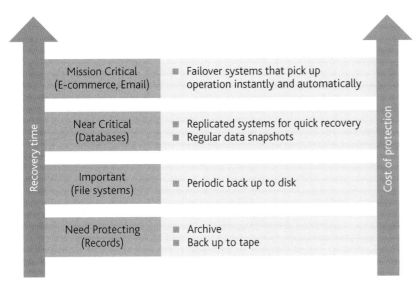

Fig. 7.4.2 *Backup methods and RTOs need to be considered alongside the importance of data to the organisation*

Making these facilities available at short notice will clearly be expensive, hence the high cost of short RTOs.

For larger scale disasters, accommodation may need to be considered. A number of options exist:

- existing accommodation: if the disaster has destroyed the system, or part of it, but left the buildings undamaged then it could be just a simple question of replacing the damaged equipment with new equipment
- alternative accommodation: if the disaster has destroyed the buildings as well as the systems (e.g. a major fire) then the first priority is to find alternative accommodation for the whole business and this should be in place as part of the disaster recovery strategy
- reciprocal site: the organisation may have made an arrangement with another organisation that have a similar system with some spare capacity
- standby site: where an organisation has a large scale system, or has sensitive data, it may not be possible to find a reciprocal partner, so a large organisation may resort to a standby site. This is obviously very expensive as it involves having a complete and up-to-date second system installed at a different location ready to be used if a disaster happens. Generally, there are two types of standby site:

– cold standby site: a site with a duplicate system, which is tested on a regular basis, but is not used unless there is a disaster

– hot standby site: where the duplicate system is up and running as a 'mirror' site processing the same live data as the main site(s) at the same time, providing a failover system

■ contract with specialist disaster recovery company: Because all of the above options involve some expense from which firms may never get a benefit (other than peace of mind), some organisations will sign a contract with a specialist data recovery company who can provide accommodation and equipment if and when it is needed. This is still expensive for the organisation, but is cheaper than providing the option themselves.

Another factor to be considered as part of a disaster recovery strategy is the risks the data and equipment will be exposed to, the likelihood of those risks occurring and the potential damage that they may inflict. The decision then has to be made as to how much the organisation is prepared to spend on recovery from those risks. The attack on the twin towers in New York invoked disaster recovery on a scale that had never been seen before and placed great pressure on available systems. Many organisations simply cannot afford to have strategies in place that will cover disasters of that magnitude.

■ **Activity**

Produce a multimedia presentation or podcast that explains the importance of backup and recovery to the management of a large organisation that would be used to support a request for funding for new disaster recovery procedures.

🔋 Backup options available for large systems

■ **Failover systems** pick up operations instantly and automatically and are vital for e-commerce operations. They immediately switch over to a standby database, server or network, depending on the nature and severity of the incident.

■ Replicated systems provide quick recovery of databases by creating a replica of each item of data as it changes so that an alternative dataset is available, perhaps on a second server.

■ Regular snapshots – snapshot is a frozen image of a file system at a given instant of time. Snapshots provide backups of the file system at several times during the day without needing large amounts of additional storage media. These provide reliable backups without the need for long backup windows and avoid the problem of files not being backed up because they are still being written to.

■ Periodic back up to disk, as it suggests involves making a backup copy to another hard disk (or disks), preferably away from the main server at intervals, depending on the frequency with which the data changes.

■ Tape backup is still a useful technique, despite the newer technologies that are now available. It allows backup to a portable medium that can be stored away from the server.

■ Archiving is useful for backing up data that may not be needed immediately but must be retained. There is no point in making constant backups of data that has not changed.

Key terms

Failover systems: used to provide continuous service for mission critical systems such as e-commerce. If the main system fails, they immediately switch to standby services to maintain continuity. They may involve standby hardware, such as a network or server, software or data, depending on the cause of the problem.

Remember

It is possible to make full, differential or incremental backups of data. These were covered in more detail in Section 14 of *AQA Information and Communication Technology AS*.

Activity

As a group, discuss the types of data that will be stored on your school or college network and list them in order of importance.

How often do you think each type of data needs to be backed up?

What do you think the RTO for each type of data should be?

What provision do you think needs to be in place if that RTO is to be achieved?

Case study

Symantec provides a variety of products, such as Backup Exec, for backing up various sizes of computer system. Their website has a series of amusing short videos covering various aspects of backup and recovery.

Go to www.symantec.com/backupexec/hal/index.jsp. Following the link to Business and resources will give you up-to-date case studies and multimedia presentations.

💡 Procedures for recovery of large scale systems

System recovery procedures provide guidance and actions for restoring the system in the event of failure, whether expected or unexpected. This means procedures for:

- identifying the facilities for providing service in the event of a failure. This might be via the organisation having a stand-by site, a reciprocal agreement with another organisation or a contract with a specialist data recovery firm
- describing the process for recovery from various types of failures
- the training of technical staff who will carry out the recovery
- planning the availability of software and operating systems needed to restore the system to operation
- planning the availability of the hardware needed to restore and run the system
- having back-up electrical power systems
- estimating the projected time for restoring the system
- testing the process of restoring the system to operation in the event of a failure
- having the appropriate documentation available.

However, with large scale information systems a partial failure is more common and the following steps would apply.

Step 1: Estimate situation

Evaluate the extent of the problem, the likely cause of the failure, the approximate amount, file types and importance of the data lost and the availability and state of the backup copies of that data, if any.

Step 2: Evaluate available resources

This includes both human and hardware resources, making sure the required expertise is available and assessing whether there is sufficient functioning hardware and hard disk space, prioritising the most critical data.

Step 3: Set up

Install good hard disks into functioning hardware and check power supply and cabling.

Step 4: Recovery run

Install the data recovery software onto the host machine and run it.

Step 5: Evaluate the results

Once the recovery is done, undertake a manual review of the most important files.

Step 6: Clean up

Remove any corrupt files or files that were created for the purpose of testing recovery.

Types of maintenance on large scale systems

After the system has been installed, the maintenance phase keeps the software up to date with environment changes and changing user requirements. Maintenance happens more efficiently if the earlier phases are done properly. If the programming has not been well structured or the system has not been well documented, maintenance becomes much more difficult.

The most likely type of maintenance to be needed when a new system is first installed is corrective maintenance to correct any errors identified during the installation process. These may be design errors, logic errors or coding errors and they prevent the software from meeting its agreed specification. These errors may remain because of a failure to test for all possible conditions, as doing this is extremely difficult in large, complex systems. A large team of maintenance engineers will need to be on hand when the system first goes live and these numbers will gradually be reduced as the system stabilises and is operating properly. Corrective maintenance should be included in the price of the original contract.

Corrective maintenance is traditional maintenance, designed to deal with errors, but there are other types of maintenance designed to help the software evolve and become more useful to the users.

Adaptive maintenance is likely to be required on a regular basis over the life of any development to keep pace with changes in its environment. These may be hardware changes, new operating systems, other software developments, security threats or changes in legislation. Some of this maintenance, for instance new security patches, will probably be included in the price of the original contract. Other changes are likely to be charged to the client. An example might be a website providing price comparisons for broadband users based on their likely usage. As conditions change, new providers come on to the market, suppliers add extra products such as TV within some of the packages. If the price comparison calculation is still to be valid, the system will need regular adaptive maintenance.

Perfective maintenance concerns functional enhancements to the system and activities to increase the system's performance or to enhance its user interface. This might be the case in generic or special purpose software, where the client has other options to move to if they feel other companies may have developed better products. The software house will be conscious of the need to make regular improvements to avoid the features in their software falling behind those of the competition. They should reflect end user feedback. For example, the interface may work adequately but if the software can be enhanced to make data entry quicker and more efficient than previously, the client will be happy and less likely to move. Examples of perfective maintenance might include adding extra report types or linking help to an online knowledge base to provide extra support.

Larger systems are likely to require more maintenance effort than smaller systems, because there are more lines of code and larger systems are more complex in terms of the variety of functions they perform.

There are several factors that are likely to make systems easier to maintain. They include:

- the use of structured techniques and standard methods
- the use of modern software – older software tends to become less organised over time, as changes are made to it
- the use of automated tools such as CASE tools
- good data administration
- experienced maintenance engineers.

There are several models for maintenance:

The quick fix model aims to identify the problem and fix it quickly, without giving much consideration to the long term effect of the fixes. This method may be acceptable in for a small system maintained by a single individual, but is not really suitable for large scale systems.

An iterative enhancement model is based on the same sort of processes used in iterative development processes. It has three stages:

- the system has to be analyzed
- proposed modifications are classified
- the changes are implemented.

This model is only effective when the documentation of the system is complete.

Maintenance teams may involve hardware and software engineers who will deal with any issues that occur initially. Every member of the maintenance team needs a comprehensive understanding of the system and may include managers, analysts, designers and programmers.

When the system is agreed to be operating at an acceptable level, it will be handed over to the client, who will then take responsibility for the day to day operation, calling on the software company via the provisions of the support contract that is in place. More details of the type of support that may be offered can be found in Section 8, Training and supporting users.

Corrective	Adaptive	Perfective
Why doesn't this work?	What about my new printer?	Wouldn't it be great if it could?

Fig. 7.4.3 *Types of maintenance*

End of sub-topic questions

5 Discuss three factors that should be considered when planning a backup strategy for a large ICT system.

6 Backing up data should ensure that data is available if a large scale organisation meeting with a major disaster such as a fire at its offices. Explain what other facilities will also need to be available for recovery and possible ways of supplying these.

☑ *In this section you have covered:*

- the effect of scale on the introduction of new systems
- the challenges posed when testing large systems
- the installation of large systems
- backup and recovery strategies
- maintaining large scale systems.

8   Training and supporting users

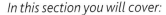
Key terms

Extranet: a section of the organisation's intranet that is available for external use, for example by suppliers or customers.

Induction training: the training carried out when a new employee joins an organisation.

Task-based training: trains the user to carry out a specific routine activity, such as filling in an on-screen data entry form or operating an EPOS checkout.

Skills-based training: aims to give the user transferable skills that can be used in a variety of ways to perform a range of functions.

In any organisation it will be both necessary and desirable to train users in order to equip them with the knowledge and skills they need to do their job effectively. Employees who undergo training are likely to experience increased job satisfaction, as they feel that they are developing within their career rather than being static.

It is also important to support users when they are doing their job in order to help them overcome any problems and difficulties they encounter.

8.1   Internal and external users

The majority of the training work carried out by organisations will be delivered to internal users – its own workforce, but there may be occasions where the training is necessary for external users who interact with the organisation, for example a supplier logging on to the organisation's **extranet**.

Types of training

When a new employee joins an organisation, they will normally undergo some **induction training**. One important part of this training will be familiarisation with the organisation's ICT policies and procedures and the importance of following them. They will also undergo **task-based training** to show them how to carry out the specific task that is required of them. For operational level users, task-based training may be all that is required to carry out specific, daily tasks, such as learning how to use the electronic point of sale terminal in a supermarket. Retraining may also be necessary if the task changes, for example when a new system is introduced.

The training of external users is likely to be task rather than skills-based, as the functionality the organisation requires them to know is likely to be extremely limited.

Training is also an important part of staff development and **skills-based training** may well be a part of this. If a person is trained to set up spreadsheets, they can use those skills in a variety of ways to carry out a variety of tasks, from keeping track of petty cash to analysing sales figures. Skills-based training tends to apply most at the tactical level of the organisation, for example a manager who needs to be able to present the results of data analysis in the most effective way. In terms of ICT functionality, strategic level managers often have other people to carry out this task for them, although some will always prefer to do their own analysis.

It may not always be practical or advisable to carry out training in one block. It is often better to do some introductory training and follow it up with further training at intervals (as in the suggested programme in Fig. 8.1.1), gradually broadening the tasks that the user can undertake without confusing them by attempting too much at once.

8.2   Training users

Cost-benefit issues

Training will always have to be justified in financial terms. For any organisation the cost of training should be seen as an investment that

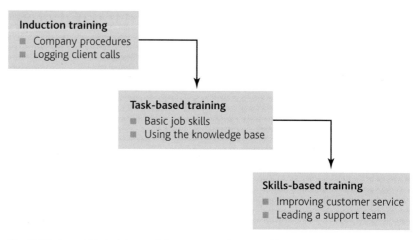

Fig. 8.1.1 *A possible training path for a new employee working on a customer support desk*

will result in some form of increased productivity and hence higher profits and the costs must always be balanced against the rewards.

In a large supermarket, or fast food outlet, for instance, there may be part-time and full-time shop floor workers or customer service assistants, for whom there tends to be quite a rapid turnover of staff. It may not be financially viable to invest a large amount in training part-time staff who may not stay in the job for very long. On the other hand, training employees may improve staff retention by improving job satisfaction. Some organisations, particularly the armed forces, insist on a minimum length of contract as a condition of providing expensive training. This enables the organisation to gain some benefit from paying for the training instead of training someone who will then move quickly to another organisation.

◪ Training methods available

Personal training

Personal training methods are ones where the user is trained by another person, either from inside or outside the organisation. This may be as part of a course or as a one-to-one session with another employee. The personal contact with the trainer is preferred by many people to learning from books or computer based training, but it does tend to cost more.

Courses

Courses can be delivered in several ways:

External course away from the organisation

Colleges and universities deliver courses that are externally verified and lead to a recognised qualification. Some organisations allow their employees regular time off to attend such courses in order to develop their knowledge and skills with a view to progressing their career within the organisation. Many of these are delivered on a part-time basis, so that an employee can study and maintain a job at the same time, although some organisations release employees for blocks of time to attend degree courses in subjects that will benefit the organisation.

Many training organisations exist who run regular courses on all sorts of topics. Most software package skills could be covered in this way and many more generic skills such as podcasting are also available. These courses typically last for one or two days at a fixed cost per person attending, which may be negotiable depending on the number of people being trained over the course of the year. If a few people need to be trained in specific areas, this may be a cost-effective way of doing so, but this tends to be uneconomical if a large number of people need to be trained.

Activity

Microsoft run training schemes and examinations that certify ICT personnel on Microsoft products at several different levels. Look at the website www. microsoft.com/learning and make notes on:

■ the types of product covered by the scheme

■ the training methods available to someone who wants to become certified on this scheme.

The fact that the employee is away from the office also needs to be considered. There will probably be travel and refreshment costs to be paid for and possibly an overnight stay for one or more nights. There may be advantages in being away from the workplace and some employees will find the change refreshing. Others may find the change in routine difficult, perhaps because of personal reasons such as child care. Some courses offer follow up opportunities, perhaps a telephone helpline open for 30 days after the course so that users requiring support when they put the course into practice have that opportunity available. The training company below use their 'Learning Port' to support users after training.

Activity

New Horizons offer training in many different packages and in many different ways. Look at their website http://learning.newhorizons.com. Compare this to the Microsoft training, including such points as:

■ the types of training provided

■ the range of training methods available

■ the levels of training available

■ the backup provided by the learning port.

In general, these courses are not tailored exactly to the needs of the organisation and this can be a disadvantage as it may not be possible to find a course that fits their requirements exactly. However, employees who attend an external course may then be able to pass on what they have learned to other colleagues, either formally or informally, a process known as 'cascading'.

External trainer delivering course within the organisation

If many people are to be trained at once, perhaps because a new system is being introduced, it may be more practical to bring the external trainer into the organisation to deliver a course that is tailored to the organisation's needs. This avoids the extra expense of travel and hotel costs, but it does mean that the company needs to provide the facilities for the course to be delivered and this may be difficult if the course is 'hands-on'. Larger companies may have training suites with computers installed or enough laptops to deliver the course in a conference room.

Everyday offices may not be suitable because of the way they are arranged and the fact that there may be other work that needs to go on while the course is being carried out.

For this type of course the organisation will pay the trainer a daily rate plus travel and expenses costs, which is likely to be cheaper than sending many employees on an external course. This type of course can usually be tailored to the requirements of the organisation and so may be more useful. It does mean that a large number of employees are unavailable for their regular duties at the same time and this may have an impact on the normal running of the organisation. However, the employees are all on site in case of urgent queries or emergencies, although unnecessary interruptions should be avoided.

Another advantage of this type of course is that the users should be able to support each other when putting into practice what they have learned and it may prove to be a useful team-building exercise.

Internal trainer

In-house training courses could also be delivered by an employee of the organisation. This may be a member of the ICT department or by an employee with specific knowledge and skills that need to be passed on. Induction training would be a good example of training likely to be given in this way. The difficulties posed by the company's training facilities are as above, but the cost of the external trainer is removed. It does mean, however, that the person delivering the training is removed from the 'day job' for the duration of the training and so there may be an impact on the organisation for that reason.

Some employees may find it difficult to deliver training to their peers and it is important that all parties concerned treat the training seriously. The person being trained may be reluctant to ask questions in this environment for fear of being seen as foolish by their colleagues, but others may find it less intimidating than being taught by a stranger. The internal trainer also has the company's interests at heart and is likely to know their requirements well.

Fig. 8.2.1 *General comparison of training courses*

One-to-one training

There are times when the best way to show someone how to do something is to sit with them while they do it. This may happen formally, perhaps as part of induction training, or informally as a person realises they need to do something they haven't done before. Provided that the two people get along, this can be a friendly and reassuring way of training someone, particularly if the user is nervous.

Personal training methods are preferred by many people because they are totally interactive. Users can ask questions and discuss difficulties and receive a personal response in a way that it is not possible to deliver by any other method. They are expensive, however, and the cost needs to be justified in terms of the benefits to the organisation.

Other methods

Online tutorials

Online tutorials are delivered via the Internet. These can be a set of step-by-step training exercises that can sometimes simulate the operation of the software. A large organisation might have sets of training packages on its own website, but more usually these training packages are provided by the software developer. If it is a specially tailored, bespoke package then the provision of online training might be included in the contract. Online training is often provided by developers of generic applications software packages. The cost of this training may be included in the price of the software or available as an optional extra that must be paid for.

The advantages for users are:

■ online tutorials are interactive and the practical nature of the tasks tends to be more interesting than paper-based tutorials would be

■ users can work at their own pace, at a time convenient to them

■ it is possible to replay the tutorials as often as the user needs to.

Online training can be cost-effective for the organisation because they can be used many times and the training that is delivered is consistent.

The main disadvantage of this method of training is that it is impersonal and the user cannot ask individual questions. There may also be a lack of impetus to complete the training, as busy users may struggle to find the time to complete the training if a specific time is not allocated for it.

Fig 8.2.2 *One-to-one training can be friendly and reassuring*

Fig. 8.2.3 *This mail merge tutorial is provided online by the software house and is accessed via the help menu on the software*

Fig. 8.2.4 *Training manuals for generic software*

Activity

Produce a tutorial for a feature of a software package with which you are familiar.

Cam studio is a free piece of open source software that allows you to record all screen activity and add an audio commentary to it. You can then save the files in avi or swf format so that the user can view them as an animated tutorial. It is downloadable from http://camstudio.org.

Training manuals

User training manuals are usually paper-based, although they may come with a CD that contains the files needed for the exercises. They may be produced by the software house that produced the software, or by a third party publisher and are widely available for popular generic packages. They tend to be based on step-by-step exercises and may have tests built in at intervals.

Advantages for the users are:

■ it is easy to select those parts of the system that the user needs to know about rather than working through all tutorials

■ the manual is always readily available for reference. For example, a senior manager who needs to use the system to produce a particular kind of report will be able to look up the required steps in the training manual.

Training manuals are generally much less expensive than training courses and for popular packages there is likely to be a good choice available. On the other hand, they are unlikely to be an option for bespoke software as they would not be economic to produce.

Some users like training manuals, but others find them more difficult to follow than electronic tutorials. It is largely a matter of personal preference.

Computer-based training (CBT)

In computer-based training the computer uses simulated versions of the software to deliver sequences of operations that the user can follow. The computer responds to user input, providing feedback and guiding the user to the next stage or asking them to repeat the current one. The software can select different pathways depending on the responses, so that the user is guided at an appropriate speed to maximise their learning. There may be built-in tests that can be marked automatically by the computer based on the responses of the user.

Some software packages also include computer-based tutorials, although they may not be quite as complex as the fully interactive versions described above. Some of these may be video-based.

As with training manuals, CBT is cheaper than courses and can be used repeatedly for many users. If it is well designed, it can respond to different levels of user depending on their responses, and so is more personalised that manuals. It still suffers from the disadvantage that the user does not have the ability to ask questions of a real human being.

Factors to be considered when choosing training:

■ how many users need training?

■ is expertise available on site?

AQA Examiner's tip

Make sure you do not get confused between **type** of training, for example induction training and **method** of training, for example internal course.

- are suitable facilities available on site?
- are external courses available?
- can existing staff be spared to train others?
- how often will staff need to be trained?
- are good quality user manuals or CBT schemes available?
- users' skill level
- users' own preferences.

End of sub-topic questions

1 Leanne has just been appointed as a customer service advisor by a high street bank. Her job will be based inside a branch advising customers about products that meet their needs and dealing with problems, queries and complaints.

a State three types of training that Leanne may need in order to do her job effectively, both initially and as her career progresses.

b For each type of training, give an example of what the training might cover and suggest a method by which the training might be delivered.

8.3 Supporting users

Anyone who uses ICT regularly, however knowledgeable or experienced, is likely to require support from time to time. With complex software operating in multi-user environments it would be surprising if things did not go wrong occasionally and users sometimes need help and reminders to carry out less familiar tasks.

Software help files

The first port of call for simple queries about software features should be the on-screen help files provided with most software. These will usually have search facilities to help the user find the information they need. Even though good software will attempt to allow the user to use **natural language** rather than technical terms, it can still be difficult to find the right section.

Did you know?

The 2003 version of Microsoft Office came with an 'Office Assistant' – an animated paper clip that bounced up and asked the question 'What do you want me to do?' A primary school child called her teacher over and said, very crossly, 'My paper clip isn't working!' Her teacher asked her what she meant and she replied 'It asked me what I wanted it to do and I typed in "Write about my summer holiday" and it hasn't done it!' Later versions of Office do not include the Office Assistant.

Key terms

Natural language interface: allows the user to ask questions in normal words rather than using technical terms. For example a user could search for 'reduce errors' rather than needing to know the term 'validation'.

Context-sensitive help: gives information based on what the user was doing when they pressed the help button.

Context-sensitive help responds to what the user was doing when help was requested. For example, if a user was attempting to set up a validated field, the help system would select pages about validation.

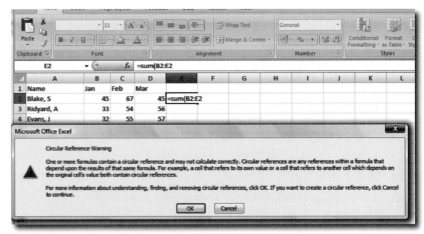

Fig. 8.3.1 *Context sensitive help responds to what the user is doing*

User guides and manuals

Fewer software packages come with printed manuals than was previously the case, and many now supply only the most basic installation on paper, preferring to include electronic versions on the media on which the software is supplied or on the support area of the company website. The user guide provides all of the technical and user documentation needed to install, maintain, run and use the software. It may also include tutorials, but on the whole user guides tend to be considered as support rather than training. Bespoke packages should also come with a user guide provided by the software house.

Whilst user guides can be useful, many people find them difficult to understand, particularly if they are not particularly strong technically. Experienced users are more likely to consult them on matters of detail, such as the syntax of a macro command.

■ Activity

Imagine you have to produce user training materials for a system you have designed and produced using a generic software package. Discuss what software you might use and the benefits and limitations of each package.

■ Key terms

Third-party manuals: are provided by publishers other than the software house that produced the software. They are generally available for popular generic software where there is sufficient market to justify their development cost.

Third-party manuals are often available at a range of levels to suit different users and may carry a mixture of training and support information. These are only likely to be available for popular generic software packages.

On site technician/help desk

Larger organisations usually have their own ICT technicians and support staff who help users through difficulties of software, hardware or both. The size of the organisation and the complexity of its ICT systems will affect the number of support staff and technicians employed by an organisation and the range of roles they are expected to carry out. In large organisations they will specialise in particular areas, but in smaller ones the technician is also likely to be the person offering support in a range of areas. Because the technical support engineers are employed by the organisation, they have its interests at heart and know a great deal about how it works. They are not trying to juggle their priorities between

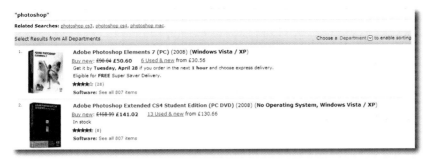

Fig. 8.3.2 *User guides are available at a range of levels to suit many users*

different customers, only between different users inside the organisation itself and being on site should also ensure a rapid response to urgent issues.

It may not be feasible or cost effective for internal support staff to handle all issues that may arise and they may still need backup from experts outside the organisation, particularly on critical components such as servers, which tend to be covered by on-site service agreements where a maximum response time is agreed and paid for.

Requests for technical support are usually logged by phone or e-mail where they are prioritised in terms of urgency and allocated to the most appropriate person. In larger organisations, the details of the problem and its solution will be logged so that they can be used as a basis for similar requests in the future.

Existing user base

Other users who already know how to use the software or hardware can be a useful source of support for users. In any organisation it is likely that if a problem occurs for a novice user, someone else in the organisation will already have met and solved it.

This can be extended to users from other organisations by the setting up of user forums on the Internet, where people can post questions and other more experienced users post possible solutions. This can be very cost effective, as such support is usually free, though some forums are run by software houses who require a fee to join.

Fig. 8.3.3 *This forum offers help with database queries*

External assistance

External helpdesk

This is a helpdesk provided by the software manufacturer, or a company with whom a support contract has been negotiated. Some software houses include technical support in the fee for the software, while others may charge by the call or by an annual fee. Organisations that operate via websites, such as UCAS, may also offer user support via helpdesks.

Contact is usually made by telephone, where details of the problem are logged. The user may get a response there and then, but often they are given a report reference number and the details of the call are fed into the system so that they can be answered by an appropriate person who will then ring the user back. Some companies operate automated telephone systems where the user chooses options on a touch-tone telephone keypad in order to reach the department they need. This may improve efficiency from the company's point of view, but can be frustrating for the user.

The user will be expected to give details of the problem and may also be asked for the serial number or licence number of the software to prove that they are authorised to receive support. They may also be asked about the operating system they are using, the hardware specification and any other software that they were running at the same time. This helps the support desk to perform some investigation before ringing back. These support desks are often located overseas now, and the levels of support they provide vary enormously (see Section 9 for further information).

Support contracts can be expensive, but they may still be more economical than paying full time staff. The response time and level of service may affect the cost.

Service contracts from software houses may include regular patches and updates to maintain the software as circumstances change. For example, payroll software will need to be updated each time tax rules change and such updates will be covered by an annual service agreement. Patches may also be needed to cover new security threats and other changes as part of the systems life cycle described in Section 6 of this book.

■ Did you know?

Customer support staff sometimes have to be extremely patient. Examples of true stories include:

Some years ago, when a customer was having trouble with his data, the engineer asked him to send a copy of the data disk (at that time, stored on a floppy disk). He did – via the fax machine!

A lady rang the support team to say thank you for helping her to back up her computer. She thought it was such a good idea, she'd now like them to help her back up the printer as well.

A little boy put his hand up in class to ask where the 'any' key was. Well, the screen did say 'Press any key to continue!'

E-mail and chat support

Some helpdesks offer support via e-mail or dedicated online chat. This tends to be a much cheaper way of offering support than a telephone response from a support engineer and many companies encourage their users to use it rather than phone. Indeed, free support services may not offer a telephone support service at all.

Remote support

As part of a support contract, some companies may set up an arrangement where they can log into the organisation's network and investigate problems and carry out solutions remotely. This can avoid a costly visit by an engineer, but it does potentially affect the level of security in the network and it is vital that the support organisation is completely trustworthy.

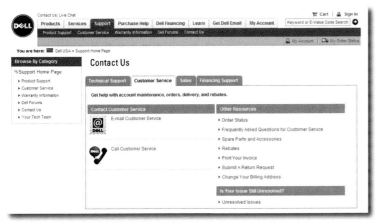

Fig. 8.3.4 *Support options accessed via company website*

Call-out support

A visit from a support engineer may sometimes be the only way to solve a problem, although it may be expensive. Some contracts include onsite service, while others charge for each visit. This may still be cheaper than employing a full-time technician if there is not enough work to justify a permanent appointment.

💡 Factors that might influence a choice of support methods

- is there enough work to justify employing support staff?
- how complex is the setup to be supported?
- how much support is provided free with software?
- how much will a support contract cost?
- what will it include?
- how quickly will support be delivered?
- are there security issues with using external contractors?

End of sub-topic questions

2 A medium-sized business organisation is considering replacing the suite of generic packages it uses for such tasks as word processing, spreadsheets and document production.

Give three alternative methods of supplying support to users of this software, together with the benefits and limitations of each method.

AQA Examiner's tip

Good answer, just not to this question!

Read the question carefully and make sure you are clear about whether the question is asking about methods for training of users or support of them. Many candidates do not do this and lose marks because they write about the wrong one.

8.4 Interfaces for customers

All organisations want to look after their customers, and one way of doing this is to make sure that interfaces are easy to use and effective so that customers do not need to be trained to use them (though they may need support from time to time).

For example, a customer wanting to withdraw money from a cash point (ATM) will not need a facility to enter lots of text or personal details, whereas someone filling in an online order form to purchase goods from an e-commerce website will need such a facility.

Where possible the interface should have a clear, simple, easy to use menu system that is intuitive to use and does not require any

Fig. 8.4.1 *An ATM screen*

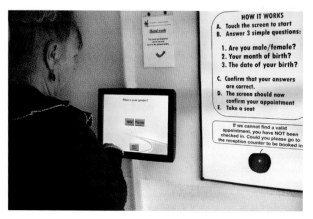

Fig. 8.4.2 *Registering Arrival Touch Screen*

Fig. 8.4.3 *IKEA allows its customers to download software to design their kitchen*

instruction. Large or multinational organisations with an international customer base may also have to consider multilingual interfaces.

Examples of customer interfaces include:

Bank customers

Bank customers can have access to their money and account information 24 hours a day, seven days a week by accessing easy to use Automatic Teller Machines (ATMs). On an ATM the main menu and each subsequent sub-menu have a limited number of options, which are selected mechanically by pressing the correct button at the sides of the screen. A key pad is provided to enter the amount of money required. Instructions on how to start are given on the screen and there may be an option for the user to select what language they prefer for their instructions, particularly in tourist areas.

Patients in a doctor's surgery

Some medical practices are equipped with a touch screen inside the waiting room where patients can register their arrival for appointments. This releases the receptionists from the mundane task of ticking them off and informing doctors of the arrivals, allowing them time to interact more fully with patients. The touch screen is linked to the computers in the doctors' offices so that the doctor knows when their patients have arrived for appointments. Each screen has a clear instruction telling the patient what to do next.

It is important that interfaces like this one, or like the ATM example listed above, are completely intuitive and require no user training whatsoever, because they will be used by many people who have no computer skills at all, have no choice but to use this method and may be anxious about having to use the technology. These interfaces are usually menu driven, with very few options available on any one screen to keep them as simple as possible.

Online shopping

A good ecommerce website will make it easy for customers to find out the information they need, choose their goods and place their order.

Some websites go even further. An example is the website for the furniture store IKEA, which allows customers to download software that enables them to design their kitchen using CAD based on standard IKEA components. The customer can choose cabinets, doors, worktops and fittings from the range and view their proposed kitchen in 3D. The software will then provide them with a complete list of all the parts they will need to build it. They can check stock availability before visiting the store or order on line if they prefer. Similar facilities are available to design offices or bedrooms.

Support for website customers tends to be simple step-by-step instructions for the functions that are available, together with Frequently Asked Questions (FAQ) to address common queries.

Managing a customer interface also involves making sure that all personnel within the organisation who have customer responsibilities are fully trained in their roles and the procedures that must be followed for dealing with customer feedback, whether it is a compliment or a complaint.

Did you know?

There are many government aided schemes for people who want to train while they work. Details of some of them are here:

www.direct.gov.uk/en/EducationAndLearning/AdultLearning/
TrainingAndWorkplaceLearning/DG_070911

In this section you have covered:

- the types of training that internal and external users may need
- training methods available
- factors to consider when selecting a training method
- the difference between training and supporting users
- methods of supporting users
- factors to consider when setting up user support
- interfaces for customer interaction.

9 External and internal resources

In this section you will cover:

- using external ICT services and business support
- managing internal resources.

9.1 External services

For a variety of reasons, it may not always be possible or desirable for an organisation to provide all of the ICT services for itself. Small businesses, for example, may have neither the time nor the expertise to do so and may choose to concentrate on their core business whilst allowing someone else to look after their ICT. In such a business, it would not be economically viable to appoint someone to a job that might only take a few hours a month but needs to be done well. It would be better to pay another organisation to handle payroll, invoicing and accounting, freeing up that time to concentrate on delivering a good service to their customers.

Specialist companies can offer a wide variety of services covering most of the functions of organisations, ranging from standard office support functions such as payroll, billing, telephone call centres, customer support, bulk printing and storage, to more specialised functions like backup and recovery.

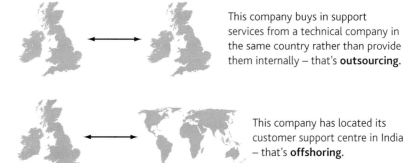

This company buys in support services from a technical company in the same country rather than provide them internally – that's **outsourcing**.

This company has located its customer support centre in India – that's **offshoring**.

Fig. 9.1.1 *Outsourcing or offshoring?*

Outsourcing

The general term for using another company to provide a service rather than providing it in house is **outsourcing**. For the purposes of your course, we are only considering the outsourcing of ICT services, although many organisations outsource other services such as cleaning and maintenance.

Reasons for outsourcing

The reasons that a company may choose to outsource are varied and may include any or all of the following:

- Improved quality – the service company will be specialists in the business functions that they are offering. They may be able to offer a level of service that would be too difficult or time consuming to develop in-house. This is more efficient than a skilled graphics artist, for example, spending lots of time on creating invoices and keeping up with the accounts which take longer because he finds it difficult or tedious.

Key terms

Outsourcing: the transfer of a function of an organisation to an external company that provides this service.

Off shoring: the transfer of an organisational function to another country, regardless of whether the work is outsourced or stays within the same corporation.

Multi-sourcing: a framework to enable services to be sourced from more than one service company.

On-demand: involves making computer resources available to the client organisation as and when needed.

Utility computing: a computing service that the customer pays for according to how much they use.

- Staffing issues – the service company would have access to a range of staff and can allocate the work to the most suitable person. The service is always available and is not going to depend on whether an individual employee is off sick or on maternity leave as it might in a small business situation.

- Capacity management – the level of service needed by the organisation may vary from month to month depending on how much work they have and the work they are doing. They can buy in extra service levels when they need it without having to employ more staff who may not always be required.

- Cost benefits – outsourcing should reduce the overall cost of the service to the business. Employing people costs more than their salary or wages, including such costs as national insurance payments, provision of sick leave or maternity benefit, and these costs are saved if work is outsourced. Similarly, specialist equipment, like large size scanners and printers, can be expensive and may not be used very often, so it may be cheaper to use a company that has the equipment in place already.

- Economies of scale – if a company produces a very large quantity of something, or does similar tasks over and over again, it is likely that the cost per unit will be lower than in a smaller operation. For example, a small or medium size business may find it is quicker and cheaper to use a bulk printing service for routine documents such as bills and payslips than it is to print them in house. The data will be transferred to the printing company via EDI, who will print and mail the documents to the required recipients.

- Reduced development time – buying in additional capability and capacity as it is needed may mean that an organisation can get a new product to the market more quickly than if they tried to do all the work themselves.

- Standardised business processes – allows a wide range of businesses access to services previously only available to large corporations.

- Improved risk management – using a specialist, for example, to advise on data backup and recovery, may reduce the risk of disastrous data loss.

Offshore provision

In certain circumstances it may prove beneficial for an organisation to use a service provider that is not based in the UK or to move certain parts of their own operation abroad. Improved global communication networks make some types of ICT provision obvious candidates to be moved offshore.

One well known and sometimes controversial use of offshore provision is the move by some large UK companies to call centres based in India rather than in the UK. Labour and facilities costs tend to be lower in India and other parts of Asia than they are in Europe and so many companies find that there are financial advantages in the move. The call centres provide valued local employment, although there have been cases of exploitation and companies using such services do not always pay the attention they should to working conditions. However, it should also be said that some companies provide good wage rates and excellent working conditions, particularly by local standards.

The map in Fig. 9.1.2 was produced in 2003. Many reports suggest that Vietnam is now the fastest growing outsourcing destination due to its low costs and high technical skills.

> **Did you know?**
>
> India's IT sector employs 1.3 million people directly, 3 million indirectly – and 40 per cent of the IT sector is concentrated in Bangalore. Bangalore also has the highest average income in India. Every Bangalore IT company has to have a private generator and uninterruptible power supply to cope with the daily power failures of the grid.
>
> *Source: news.bbc.co.uk*

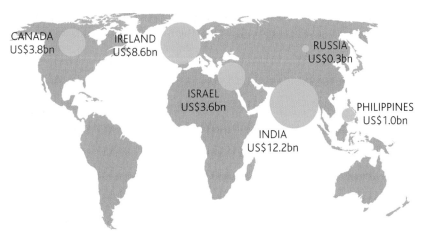

CANADA
US$3.8bn

IRELAND
US$8.6bn

RUSSIA
US$0.3bn

ISRAEL
US$3.6bn

PHILIPPINES
US$1.0bn

INDIA
US$12.2bn

Fig. 9.1.2 *Top countries for global IT outsourcing*

Some customers have proved extremely hostile to the move. In general, if a customer has to contact customer support, they are unhappy with the company's service in some way. If they are then faced with a long wait in a telephone queue, their stress levels will be increasing and by the time they get through to the operator they may start off in a less than positive frame of mind, occasionally resulting in rude or abusive behaviour. Difficulties with accents, a lack of local knowledge and perhaps under-trained employees relying totally on scripts from a knowledge-based system will not help the situation and in this scenario the experience is almost bound to be a negative one.

In call centres where the operators are well trained and speak clearly, the question of where the operator is physically located should be much less of an issue, but some companies make a particular point, in their advertising material, of declaring that all their call centres are UK based, because they feel that is a major selling point with some customers. Other companies are using a compromise solution by using offshore centres for routine calls and UK based ones for more complex enquiries that are likely to involve a significant amount of discussion. This process is known as 'rightshoring' and estimates indicate that about 80 per cent of organisations in Britain split their call-centre operations in this way. Supporting customers via e-mail and chat may also reduce the difficulties posed by language and dialects.

Call centres are by no means the only ICT facility where off shore provision has become popular. Specialist technical skills, such as programming, are also often cheaper to obtain abroad and the communication difficulties that affect call centre operations are much less evident here, as the customer has no direct contact with the offshore utility and it is easier to employ multilingual staff to liaise between countries.

Some bodies in the UK, for example trade unions, are concerned about the move to offshore operations, fearing its impact for UK jobs and rates of pay. Other people feel that if living standards across the world can be improved, the global markets become larger and more people can afford to buy things, and everybody benefits.

In practice, organisations may use a combination of methods and suppliers to obtain their ICT services. They may outsource to several companies, some of whom may use offshore services as part of their provision. They may set up an offshore operation to provide some services and that offshore company may, in turn, outsource within their own country. What is important is that the standard of products and services delivered to the parent company remains high and this will be in jeopardy if the situation is not carefully managed and monitored.

◥ *Benefits and limitations of offshore provision*

- labour and facilities may be cheaper abroad, resulting in cost savings
- specialist skills may be more readily available, again at lower costs
- some countries may offer financial incentives to encourage new business
- the jobs and investment may be extremely valuable to the local economy
- assists the global economy by providing work to less wealthy areas of the world
- language and cultural differences may cause difficulties
- communications costs may be higher
- legislation may be different abroad and so it is important to ensure that, for example, rights under the Data Protection Act are not breached
- security risks may be increased as the organisation moves away from local control.

End of sub-topic questions

1 Describe the difference between outsourcing and offshore provision, giving an example of an ICT service that might be provided by each method.

2 A local building firm consists of the owner and three skilled building tradesmen. Suggest two aspects of the business that might be best provided by outsourcing to an ICT company, giving reasons for your choice.

AQA Examiner's tip

Make sure when you answer questions on topics such as outsourcing that you frame your answer in an ICT context. For example, a hospital may choose to outsource its catering supplies, but that is not relevant here. A software company outsourcing its customer support would be a much better example.

9.2 Ways of obtaining services

There are a number of different ways in which organisations can obtain external services from suppliers or service companies. Depending on the specific service these can include:

- **buying** hardware, software and equipment
- **contracting** people, work space and equipment
- **leasing** software, communication links and equipment.

Buying

Buying hardware, software and equipment requires a high level of initial investment, which may take several years to pay for itself. The items bought do become assets for the company, but in practice are likely to have limited resale value given the speed with which technology changes. The cost of the equipment spread over several years is likely to be less than contracting or leasing, but arrangements have to be made for support, servicing and maintenance, which may be included in other methods. If the company has to borrow money to finance the initial investment, interest charges also need to be taken into account. For these reasons, many organisations choose to use other methods of obtaining services.

Contracting

Contracting involves making an agreement with a supplier to provide a specific service for a specific period of time at an agreed cost. The contract may be agreed on a monthly or annual basis, or for a fixed term or for a specific job. For example, a company could pay a data warehouse on a monthly basis to back up its data and maintain a copy away from company premises. They may be able to negotiate a lower price if they agree to a longer term, such as two years rather than one. The contract is likely to specify how much data is included in the price and extra charges may be levied if the volume of data exceeds the limit.

The same company could also set up a fixed term contract for a network manager, perhaps to cover maternity leave or because of increased demand over a short period. The contractor would not have the same employment rights as a full time employee, but their rate of pay may be higher and they may be self-employed or work through an employment agency. Many companies use employment agencies to supply temporary staff, because it means they do not have to spend time advertising and interviewing for themselves.

The company could also take on a contract, which means that they will need extra staff to cover them for the additional work brought in by that contract. Those staff would be given employment contracts that last for the duration of the company's contract. The same options could also apply to office space and equipment, which may only be needed for a limited period of time due to short term demand.

Contracting can also be an important part of a company's disaster management strategy. In the event of a major catastrophe such as a fire, a company may need office space, computers and staff in order to recover their data and operations to a different location. They can take out a contract that makes these facilities available in order to get the operation up and running in the shortest possible time. These provisions may not be perfect, because the company providing the facilities will work on the assumption that not all the companies they have contracts with will need the equipment at the same time. In most cases, this will be true, but in the, fortunately rare, event of a major disaster, provision may not be adequate. This caused major problems in the aftermath of the twin towers attacks in New York.

Case study: disaster recovery

Disaster recovery lessons from the World Trade Centre

Two law firms, both just a few blocks away from the World Trade Center, were equally decimated by the collapse of 1.8 million tons of glass and steel on September 11. Both firms used the same company to help them reconstitute business, but one firm was up and back to business as usual in two days. The other lost everything and, a year later, is still in the process of digging through paper files in warehouses, going back to clients and even competitors to try and recreate its records.

So goes an anecdote from Andrew Kass, director of technical services for Array Technologies, the New York-based consulting firm that helped the two law firms with their disaster recovery plans. Law firm A had followed his company's prescriptions to the letter, while firm B had used some of Array's services for its networking and documentation, but had taken matters into its own hands on business continuity matters, making the unwise-and ultimately unlucky – decision to store their backup tapes in the World Trade Center.

The interview continues ...

'What are the most important lessons would you say that you – or the industry overall – learned about disaster recovery practices from 9/11?'

Kass: For companies directly impacted, the three keys were backup, re-staging and lighting up or improvising new infrastructure services. A lot of companies that spent thousands on hot sites got short shrift when the sites were swamped and no one was flying. And for most downtown businesses, electricity and phone service, let alone Internet connectivity, were huge X factors for months following the attack.

I think hot-site centres proved less valuable than anticipated – they just couldn't scale space to this huge and sudden demand. Virtual office strategies – mirrored data centers with remote VPN access – offer a more flexible and serviceable approach leveraging the recoverability and versatility of the Internet, with fewer worries about bathrooms and parking.

Source: www.zdnet.co.uk

Leasing

As an alternative to purchasing, companies may decide to enter into a leasing agreement for their hardware, software or communications facilities.

If equipment or software is leased rather than purchased, the company does not own it outright. Instead, they pay a monthly fee to use it. Leasing agreements mean that the initial investment is not as high as it would be if the equipment was purchased and there may be further benefits included in the price. For example, if a company chooses to lease rather than buy its software, the agreement will usually include support services and regular upgrades. This makes financial planning easier as

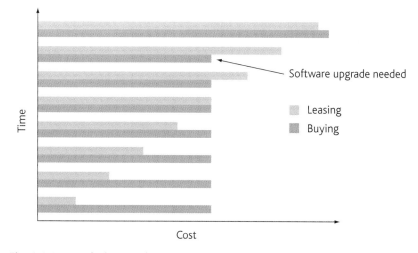

Fig. 9.2.1 *Costs for leasing v buying software*

companies know that there will not be any single substantial investments needed to keep abreast of new releases, with costs for this spread into more manageable chunks included as part of the leasing agreement. The overall cost may be higher, but it is spread out.

Leasing arrangements may also apply to communications facilities. Leasing a dedicated line over which to run the company's network may be appealing to companies that operate from more than one geographical location and so need a WAN rather than just a LAN. This is likely to give them a more secure connection and better data transfer speeds than may be achievable over a normal shared connection from a telephone supplier.

Leasing evens out costs, but may cost more overall.

9.3 Managing internal resources

Any organisation has internal resources that must be managed and controlled. These include:

- people
- hardware resources
- software resources
- communication resources
- consumables
- facilities
- power.

Previous chapters have looked at the importance of ICT strategies and policies to any organisation and these will be important tools in the management of its internal resources.

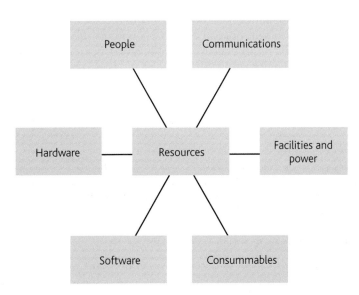

Fig. 9.3.1 *Internal resources*

People

The Human Resources or Personnel department will be largely responsible for the management of the people who work within an organisation. They will be involved in new appointments, staff development and pastoral care of employees and responsible for overseeing disciplinary procedures and their implementation. When a new employee is appointed, they will sign a contract of employment and this will make reference to the security and acceptable use policies, plus any other policies or procedures that the employee is expected to follow. Disciplinary procedures can be used to deal with breaches of these policies.

On a more positive note, training and staff development will also be important, and a major factor in staff loyalty and staff retention. Replacing staff who leave is time consuming and can be expensive in terms of advertising and interviewing and so investing in existing staff can make financial as well as moral sense.

Temporary staff, contracted directly or through an agency, will also need to be managed and it is important that they too are aware of the policies and procedures with which they must comply.

As explained in Section 2, HR management software can be used to help with these functions.

Hardware resources

Computer hardware is an expensive and continuous investment, and it is important that its purchase and use is controlled. Procurement policies will govern the way hardware is purchased or leased, but it is equally important to track what happens to it once it has been obtained. An asset register is a useful tool in terms of managing hardware. This involves using a database to store details of each piece of hardware, its location and its technical specification. Any faults, repairs and upgrades can be added to the record, allowing the ICT department to be able to evaluate what equipment they have and what may need upgrading or replacement in the near future. This can help with budgeting, and is an important record to have for accounting and insurance purposes.

The network operating system will also monitor some hardware items, such as hard disks and show error messages if problems seem to be developing. It also has accounting features that can produce reports on how much disk space is being used by any particular user or department and can set quotas that restrict the maximum amount of disk space a user is allowed.

Uninterruptible power supplies can be fitted to important hardware devices, such as servers, in order to protect them in the event of a power failure. They can also be used to monitor the power that is supplied to them, producing charts or tables of voltages. This can be a useful diagnostic tool to check whether power surges or drops in voltage are being experienced by the hardware. Surge protectors can also be fitted to protect against voltage spikes.

Software resources

Asset management software may also record the software that is installed on each machine, but there are other tools that will help with software management. Licence management software is available that will monitor the software installed on each workstation on the network, together with its version. This is an important tool for compliance with the Copyright and Patents Act.

Another way of maintaining control over software is to install it on the server rather than on each client workstation. This can also be set up in such a way that makes software use for a given number of licences a little more flexible. If a company has a licence for 25 users of a particular piece of software but has 100 workstations, it can install the software on 25 workstations. If they are installed on the server, provided it is controlled properly, at can be used on any 25 workstations provided no more than 25 copies are in use at any one time. If a 26th person tries to use the software, it will not load, thus making sure that the licence terms are abided by.

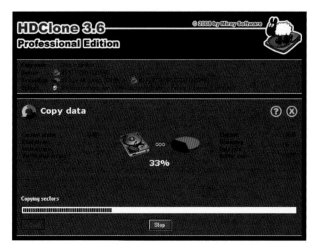

Fig. 9.3.2 *Cloning software allows an entire hard disk to be copied*

Tools can also be used by network managers and technicians to deal with software installation and upgrades, which can be time consuming to roll out to all the machines on a large network. Cloning software allows a technician to take an image of a hard disk and copy it to many more rather than have to install all the software on each disk individually. Additionally, network versions of virus checking software can be set up in such a way that each workstation updates its virus definitions as soon as it is switched on.

Communication resources

Network management software can produce diagnostic reports on network traffic that should indicate if the number of collisions on the network is rising above acceptable levels, which may indicate communication link problems.

Filtering software can be used to prevent access to certain types of site on the Internet. One reason for this may be to conserve the available bandwidth and ensure it is used for approved company purposes. The filters may be set to block sites that provide streaming media such as music, radio and video. If lots of people want to listen to music while they work or keep an eye on the cricket scores by leaving live coverage running it can soon have a detrimental effect on network performance. Social networking sites are also banned by many organisations as are sites containing pornographic, racist or other inappropriate content.

Setting up a proxy server can help an organisation protect its communication systems and may also improve speed. It sits between the users and the Internet and when users request a web page, the request goes first to the proxy server and from there to the web server. The only IP address visible to the web server is that of the proxy server, which is of much less use to a hacker than the IP address of an individual machine. The fact that common web pages are cached on the proxy server will make them quicker to load.

Did you know?

Some reports claim that up to two-thirds of businesses are now banning social networking sites.

Activity

Asset tracking software can help organisations control the use of their ICT facilities.

The website www.resourcemonitor.com gives one example. The website www.novell.com/products/zenworks/assetmanagement gives another, including a webcast demo.

Imagine you are an ICT manager for a large organisation. Produce a report to the directors that would make a case for buying asset tracking software.

Consumables

Network management software can control which users have access to which printers and print accounting software can be used to control the amount of printing done by any user or department. It can keep track of how many pages any user has sent to any printer and charges can be calculated based on price per page.

Activity

Kyocera Mita (www.kyoceramita.co.uk) is a company that produces laser printers. They market their products as economical to run and environmentally friendly. Their website includes a facility to compare the running costs of different brands of laser printer.

1 Sum up the steps that Kyocera are taking to reduce the environmental impact of their printers.

2 Use the calculator provided on the site to model the running costs of two similar printers. Investigate the effect of :

- quantity of copies per month
- time – check the figures over 1, 2 and 3 years
- coverage – compare 5 per cent and 15 percent coverage for different types of document.

Remember

Printer toner can be harmful to your health and great care should be taken to follow the instructions when cartridges are changed.

Many organisations accept toner and inkjet cartridges for recycling and this should be encouraged.

Facilities and power

Power consumption should be considered when new equipment is purchased and all users should be encouraged to switch off workstations at the end of the working day rather than leave them in standby mode to save power. All computers should have a power saving mode that the computers go into if they have not been user after say 20 minutes.

End of sub-topic questions

3 Explain why the use of ICT equipment can have negative effects on the environment and suggest strategies that organisations can adopt to reduce their environmental impact.

✔ *In this section you have covered:*

- the fact that organisations may choose to obtain some ICT services externally
- outsourcing and the reasons organisations might decide to use it
- offshoring and the reasons organisations might choose to obtain services abroad
- bulk printing services and economies of scale
- contracting and leasing arrangements and why they may be useful
- planning and managing internal resources such as people, hardware, software, communications, consumables, facilities and power.

10 Future developments

Fig. 10.1.1 *EPOS systems have changed the way people shop and given retailers better information*

Did you know?

In 1943, Thomas Watson, then the chairman of IBM, is reported to have said: 'In the whole world there is a market for maybe five computers.'

10.1 Emerging technologies

In the beginning

ICT has always been the focus of rapidly-moving technologies and by its very nature that makes it difficult to keep up with:

- The manufacturing industry has always looked for quicker and more efficient ways to make things and has developed computer-aided design and manufacture.

- Governments and organisations have needed ways to collect and analyse data and so have developed new data capture methods and powerful databases.

- Retail organisations needed to process customer purchases quickly and use data about shoppers to improve their profitability.

- Scientific organisations have needed to carry out complex calculations on large amounts of data and have developed computers with powerful processors and large amounts of memory and storage space.

- Businessmen and women have needed ways to keep in touch when they were away from the office, and the mobile devices they demanded have now been adopted by lots of other people.

Major Impacts

So what has made these developments possible?

- the reduction in size of devices enabled first by transistors and then by micro circuitry

- the increase in processing power so that modern supercomputers have processing speeds of over 1 teraflop – 10^{12} (i.e. one million million) operations per second

- the development of new methods of storage, such as flash memory, that enable increased portability

- advances in telecommunications that have allowed data to be transferred almost instantly across the world and locally between wireless devices.

These technologies have emerged and made change possible and newer technologies will continue to do so.

Mobile working

For a long time now, businesses have wanted to keep in touch with their employees wherever they were working, whether it was to tell an electrician that they needed to move to an emergency job or to send an urgent report to a director on a visit abroad. That need has driven the development of portable computers and mobile phones and still continues to do so.

Only a few years ago a business traveller would have carried a laptop for producing documents, a mobile phone for making calls and a PDA for short notes and contact information. The laptop would be connected via a landline and a modem to send documents back and forth to the office.

In recent years it has become much more difficult to give modern mobile devices a name. Phones are also digital cameras, address books, music and video players, notebooks and a means of connecting to the Internet. These are features that until recently would have only been found in laptops or PDAs. These devices are now converging, as people increasingly look to carry a single device rather than a whole briefcase full!

Compared to the early models, phones became smaller and smaller. However, whilst they were fine as phones, users found them difficult to use for web surfing, reading and producing documents. As a result of this, many phones have become larger again as the use of tiny keyboards and touch screens enable people to send e-mail, surf the Internet, play music or watch TV programmes.

Fig. 10.1.2 *Is it a phone? Is it a PDA? Is it a computer?*

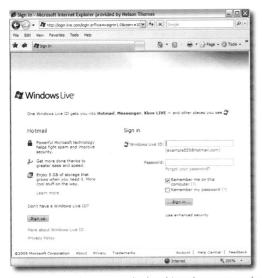

Fig. 10.1.3 *A laptop can display this web page completely, whereas the mobile user will need to scroll*

This conflict between reduction in size and ease of use is one that computer companies are working hard to overcome and the development of user interfaces that are both useable and portable is a major area of research. Visual output becomes unusable below a certain size, because so little of the page can be shown at once or text becomes too small to read and not all output is suitable for transmission via sound. Similarly, while the need to enter data via a real or virtual keyboard exists, the user needs to be able to see and touch the keys. Voice recognition is gradually improving, but is not necessarily the answer for communications that need to be kept private.

Activities

1 Consider all of the functions of a modern mobile device. Make a list of all the things a person would have had to carry 10 years ago if they wanted to carry out the same functions.

2 Do some background research on mobile interface design. Small Surfaces is a site about design for mobile technology. This site tracks articles about interaction design, user interface design, user experience, usability and social trends related to mobile devices and is a good place to start (www.smallsurfaces.com). Produce a short presentation about the most interesting things that you found out.

Did you know?

Many popular websites such as eBay produce versions of their sites that are designed to work on mobile devices. The mobile version of eBay splits the main page into tabbed pages to streamline what you see and allow it to fit on the screen better. The mobile site mirrors the main one so bidding is kept up to date. Find out more on http://pages.ebay.com/mobile/mobileweb.html

Entertainment

The convergence experienced in mobile devices is also happening in home entertainment, where digital data enables users to listen to music, watch TV and take part in interactive programmes, and this is a trend that is likely to increase and develop in the 21st century. TV schedules are increasingly becoming a matter of the user's preference rather than the TV companies, as content is provided for people to download and view at their own convenience. It has become far easier and cheaper to set up a television station – look at how many football teams have their own channels. This gives them a great deal of control over their marketing and the experience of their fans.

Sites like YouTube, in enabling people to share their music with others, changed the way that music companies recruit. Instead of acts having to trail demo tapes around record companies, they increasingly post their performances online and the best develop a fan base there. This is particularly appropriate as more and more music and video is downloaded rather than purchased on media through high street stores.

Activity

Look at www.ukmusic.org – which gives lots of information about music trends. The 'press releases' and 'articles' links will give you up to date information about issues relating to music, such as a survey by British Music rights on the music consumption behaviour and experience of young people aged 14–24.

Write a short summary of what you think are the most important issues and trends. You could compare that to the behaviour of your own friends by carrying out a survey.

Fig. 10.1.4 *The Optoma Pico is digital projector about the same size as a mobile phone*

Did you know?

Ken Olson, President, Chairman and Founder of Digital Equipment Co. in 1977 made the statement: 'There is no reason anyone would want a computer in their home.'

For some performers this has encouraged a new spirit of cooperation and Creative Commons is a form of copyright that allows people to use music, photographs or video created by other people under certain conditions as opposed to the 'all rights reserved' approach adopted by most creators of media. Performers can produce collaborative projects without even being in the same country!

http://creativecommons.org/ explains more about Creative Commons, including a slide show to explain the idea. An example of its use is given at: http://www.mobygratis.com/film-music.html, where non-commercial film makers can use Moby's music without paying a fee.

Visual media stored on a mobile device can now be projected onto a large surface, such as a folding screen or even a white wall, via a pocket-sized digital projector. This makes business and personal video and photo displays much more portable than they were previously.

Ubiquitous computing

The most profound technologies are those that disappear. They weave themselves into the fabric of everyday life until they are indistinguishable from it.

Mark Weiser, 'The Computer for the 21st Century' in: Scientific American 265, *Nr. 3, S. 94–101*

The idea of ubiquitous computing is that users interface with a range of devices that work together seamlessly without the user being conscious of it. In some ways, that is the natural extension of the ideas on convergence that we have already considered. It involves removing the barriers that make devices difficult to use and making them work for the user. Clothes, for example, could have tags that are read by a washing machine so that it automatically knows how to wash them.

As more and more items become able to connect, the possibilities for interactivity grow. Each item to be connected would need an individual ID, provided by a RFID (Radio Frequency Identification) tag. RFID tags in mobile phones, for example, could be used to pay for goods, just as the Oyster card is currently used on the London Underground.

Another possibility for identification is a visual bar code, or 'tag' – a printed picture containing data that can be photographed just as traditional bar codes are. Semacode tags can be downloaded and printed from the Semacode website (www.semacode.com) for any URL, and they can be captured by a mobile phone camera. Here is a quote from their website: 'Semacode uses 2D barcodes as a physical world hyperlink. Our software provides the infrastructure to allow any cell phone to do a one click purchase, one click coupon, one click download, one click customer service. A Semacode gives any website a tangible physical presence, one that can be acted upon by users impulse anywhere. A Semacode is a barcode, a two-dimensional created code, a registered word, a fingerprint. Don't think of a barcode as a barcode, imagine it's a web address and your cell phone's browser works just by clicking on it. No need to type the web address in, just click on it.'

Other companies are currently making similar devices.

The fact that modern technology can identify the position of things using **GPS (Global Positioning System)** technology means that mobile phones, and even school bags, could be tracked. Schools and colleges could use these to keep people and their belongings safe, but there are also potential issues of personal privacy. Just think, this technology could mean you never lose anything ever again, but on the other hand you could be tracked everywhere you go! The same technology could link mobile phones to advertising or other information signs, downloading data to provide the user with information about the product or service.

These are small examples, but ubiquitous computing relies on an increasing number of devices being able to connect to each other, often without the human being even being aware that they are doing so.

Fig. 10.1.5 *RFID transponder*

Fig. 10.1.6 *Semacode tag to Nelson Thorne's website*

 Did you know?

People have started printing semacode tag patterns on t-shirts. Other people can photograph them with their phone and then link to the url that is coded. This could be their website or social networking page.

 Key terms

GPS technology: global positioning system technology tracks the position of objects using satellites.

 Did you know?

Create-a-scape (http://createascape.org.uk/) allows schoolchildren to create their own mediascapes, recording sound, pictures and video that are attached to a digital map of the local area and can be played back by a user following the trail with a hand held computer and headphones. GPS technology means that the correct clip is automatically played at the correct location.

 PC activity

Look at the create-a-scape website. How could you see such technology being used in education and in the leisure industry?

 End of sub-topic questions

1 Global Positioning Satellites (GPS) can now be used to find the location of a mobile phone. This is very useful to car breakdown organisations if you are unsure of where you are when you have broken down. Describe some other positive or negative implications of this use of technology.

Key terms

Supercomputers: are mainframe computers that are amongst the most powerful computers at any particular time.

10.2 Potential future uses of ICT

Supercomputers

The most powerful computers in the world are knows as **supercomputers.** These computers are mainframes and are designed to carry out calculations extremely quickly. Their speed is measured in flops (floating point operations per second) and in 2008, the world's first petaflop computer was announced (one quadrillion floating point operations per second). Road runner, as the computer is nicknamed, was built by IBM for the US Department of Energy's Los Alamos National Laboratory. It will be used, amongst other things, for modelling how nuclear materials age – to try to minimise the dangers presented by nuclear waste.

Other supercomputers are used to model weather and climate, to investigate the performance of new drugs, or even to work out why crisps keep getting blown off a production line!

The Top 500 list is published twice a year and lists the top 500 computers in terms of performance, together with their technical specifications and the area in which they are being used. The list and further information can be found at www.top500.org.

PC activity

Using the Top500 site, or any news article you can find, produce a newsletter that gives details of a current supercomputer that is working in an area that interests you.

Did you know?

Researchers in the Human Interface Technologies Team at the University of Birmingham are developing computer simulations that are more realistic by using the sense of smell. Soldiers headed for the Middle East will be able to experience what it might be like on the ground by walking past objects displayed on large screens and experiencing the smells at the same time. Soldiers can expect to sniff aromas including body odour, sewage, rotting vegetable, spices and gunshot in an attempt to create an immersive environment where the whole situation feels real. Nobody is certain yet how useful this feature will be, or whether it will make a difference to the trainees' experiences. The technology is likely to be extended to video games within a few years.

www.iecs.bham.ac.uk/hit/ gives more information about the human interface team and its work.

Brain-controlled computing

Human brain activity is made up of electrical signals and so the possibility of using brain waves to control devices is moving out of the realms of science fiction. An Austrian company is developing an interface that uses a cap containing electrodes that rest on the scalp of the user. The electrodes monitor tiny changes in electrical voltages and the system interprets them via software in an attempt to identify what the user is thinking. The software has to be 'trained' to interpret the signals correctly, and at present is very slow, but the possibilities are enormous, particularly for people with disabilities. Invasive technology, where the receptors would be implanted inside the brain would produce more reliable results, but many people would feel very nervous about such a development. In fact, most people would feel very nervous about any system that always knew what they were thinking!

End of sub-topic questions

2 What, if any, are the implications for the security of ICT systems and data, of using thought to access systems?

3 Describe what, if any, new legislation might be needed if it were possible to transmit thoughts directly between people.

10.3 Implications of future developments

Mobile working

The advent of communication technologies such as WiFi, Bluetooth and mobile broadband have transformed the way that people work and do business. Most people are easy to contact in any number of ways and so the need to be physically present in an office every day has become less important. As the use of teleworking and videoconferencing increases, the need to travel should reduce and consequently the environmental impact of business journeys should reduce. These developments make it increasingly easy for organisations to recruit teams from all over the world to work together on projects.

On the other hand, it may also mean that people's stress levels rise as it becomes increasingly difficult to escape and relax. Security also becomes of great concern when financial transactions are carried out on tiny devices using wireless communication. Business data is also potentially at risk as so much of it can be accessed from and stored on small, portable devices.

Bioinformatics

One major area of scientific research in the 21st century is bioinformatics. Since the human genome project was completed in 2003, scientists have continued to investigate the 20,000 or more genes in human DNA and computer databases play a major part in this work. This area of science explores the effect of these genes on human health, enabling scientists to identify hereditary traits and predict the likelihood of future illnesses. Due to the obvious potential for such technology to be used to identify people who are poor risks from an employment or life insurance point of view – in 2008 the American Congress passed an act to prohibit discrimination on the basis of genetic information with respect to health insurance and employment.

Activity

In small groups, discuss the potential impact of bioiformatics on society. If you could be given information about your future health based on your DNA profile, would you want it? Should that information be available to anyone other than the individual themselves? Should DNA information about an unborn child be available to its parents?

Interplanetary Internet?

We are used to using the Internet to communicate between networks using protocols. Though still in the study stage, NASA is considering setting up the capability for the various unmanned probes that populate the surface of the moon to communicate with each other and to send data to computers back on Earth. One major problem that still has to be overcome is supplying the probes with power. Some of the probes could be in darkness for 14 days at a time, so solar power is not really feasible. Nuclear power is also being considered. The project is called the International Lunar Network or ILN. For more details, look on the NASA website (www.nasa.gov).

AQA Examiner's tip

The A2 examination emphasises the effect of emerging technologies on business, organisations and society, rather than just on individuals. Specific technologies may be mentioned in case studies, which you will be given time to research.

End of sub-topic questions

Let's pretend

4 Imagine that technological improvements have enabled images to be produced in the air around us without needing a physical display device. The images can be two- or three-dimensional and they could be linked to sound, so it would be possible to create a virtual person in the room

where the user is sitting. The use of 3-D body scanners to create that image would mean that a person could visit other people virtually, without having to travel there physically. Objects could be created in the same way and placed in a person's house or office.

Discuss the potential implications of the use of this technology, including:

■ commercial opportunities for businesses

■ the impact this could have on society or individuals

■ ithat may require new legislation

■ ethical issues that the technology might create.

⚡ Keeping up

By its very nature, ICT technology moves too quickly for a book like this to keep up with and the subject is too huge to cover in any depth at all. You should try to keep in touch with the latest developments by watching news programmes and shows such as *The Gadget Show* that deal with new developments.

Online newspapers and magazines are also good sources of information and many of them allow you to set up RSS feeds that deliver the news to your desktop without you having to remember to look for it.

☑ *In this section you have covered:*

■ some of the technologies that are emerging at the beginning of the 21st century

■ potential uses of new technological developments

■ the importance of considering the impact of new technologies on businesses, organisations and society

■ the fact that new technologies may bring ethical and moral dilemmas

■ the importance of keeping yourself up to date with the latest developments.

Special effects company: a case study

Fxontap is a new company specialising in special effects for film, video and computer game companies. The company has recording studios for audio and video, plus editing suites and conference rooms for discussions with clients. Their expertise is in special effects animation based on footage recorded in the studios, which is then edited and combined with computer graphics to produce the spectacular effects for which they have become famous. They have recently taken over a converted warehouse building on the canal side in Birmingham. The warehouse is a listed building and so they have decided to install a wireless rather than a cabled network.

The company employs graphics artists from all over the UK who work partly from home and partly in the office, depending on what stage any project is at. The network allows remote access by the employees, as does the extranet. The artists all have laptops as well as desktop computers at home, and the office operates a hot desking policy using workstations that have docking facilities for laptops.

The company have decided to invest in a new system to improve the accessibility of their media library and enable artists to search for media files that they might be able to incorporate in new projects. The artists work in teams and good communication and project management is essential if projects are to be delivered on time.

The other major computer investment is an administration system that combines human resources, financial management and payroll. This system replaces an older personnel system database and payroll system. They hope the new system will help them allocate new projects more efficiently to the correct designers by tracking success rates on various types of project. Workflow management is extremely important to the company as they are managing large numbers of projects that place heavy demands on human skills and specialist facilities.

Section 1: Information

1   The owner of an independent health club, that employs six instructors, decides to get a local software house to produce a customised database to manage client data including the booking of sessions, the tracking of progress and the recording of payments.

    (a)   Identify two different potential users of this system who are at different levels within the organisation. *(2 marks)*

    (b)   With the aid of examples, describe the different levels of information that each of these two users might require. *(6 marks)*

2   A high-street building society uses a data processing system to record receipts and withdrawals from its customers' accounts. The data from branches are sent once a day up to the ICT systems at head office in Yorkshire to update all master accounts and all data is then input into various management information systems.

    (a)   For each of the following users, state the level of information that is needed by:

        (i)   a Customer Service Clerk in a local branch *(1 mark)*

        (ii) a Branch Manager *(1 mark)*

        (iii) the Managing Director of the building society. *(1 mark)*

    (b)   For each of the following individuals, name a suitable output, state how it may be used, and give a typical item of data that it may contain.

        (i)   a Customer Service Clerk in a local branch *(3 marks)*

     (ii) a Branch Manager *(3 marks)*

     (iii) the ICT Manager, controlling all ICT systems within the building society *(3 marks)*

     (iv) the Managing Director of the building society. *(3 marks)*

  (c)   Explain why the information used by the Customer Service Clerk is not appropriate for the Managing Director. *(3 marks)*

AQA, 2006

3   Information produced by ICT systems may be required both within (internal) and outside (external) organisations such as schools and supermarkets.

  (a)   Describe two examples of internal information requirements, stating for each:

     (i)   who needs the information

     (ii) what information they require

     (iii) what it is to be used for. *(6 marks)*

  (b)   Describe two examples of external information requirements, stating for each:

     (i)   who needs the information;

     (ii) what information they require;

     (iii) what it is to be used for. *(6 marks)*

AQA, 2005

▦ Section 2: Systems

1   When buying concert tickets over the Internet from an online booking system, customers access the company's booking and payment systems.

  (a)   Describe three different methods the customer might choose from to pay for the tickets. *(6 marks)*

  (b)   Good quality information is vital to both the online booking company and its customers.

     (i)   Explain, giving an example, what good information means in this context. *(2 marks)*

     (ii) Describe **two** benefits to the company of using e-commerce for this operation. *(2 marks)*

     (iii) Explain how the data captured in these transactions may be used in other systems within the organisation. *(4 marks)*

2   A team of authors are writing a set of training resources that will be published on the intranet of a large multi-national company. Each resource will need to be edited and approved before it can be published. Some resources will require research based on publications the company has already produced.

Discuss the ICT systems that can be used to manage this work effectively. *(8 marks)*

▦ Section 3: Management and strategies

1   Describe four reasons why a large organisation should have a corporate ICT strategy. *(12 marks)*

2   When writing a corporate information systems strategy for an organisation, various factors have to be taken into account, including the structure of the organisation.

Give **five** other factors that might be considered when writing a Corporate Information Systems Strategy and, for each one, give a reason why it might be considered. *(10 marks)*

AQA, 2007

3   Information flows within an organisation by both formal and informal mechanisms.

  (a)   What is meant by formal information flow? Give an example of a formal information flow mechanism. *(3 marks)*

(b)   What is meant by informal information flow? Give an example of an informal information flow mechanism.   *(2 marks)*

AQA, 2006

Section 4: Policies and legislation

1   (a)   An engineering company has purchased a design package with a licence agreement that allows up to 10 users at any one time. The company computer network has over 100 terminals and an engineer may need to use the design package at any terminal. Describe one way of installing this package that will ensure the company does not break its licence agreement.   *(2 marks)*

(b)   Describe two actions that the company could take to discourage or prevent the installation of unauthorised software on its network.   *(4 marks)*

AQA, 2007

2   'An organisation's data is its most important asset.' Discuss this statement, with regard to:

(a)   The importance of data to organisations.

(b)   The role of security policies in maintaining the security and privacy of data.

(c)   The reasons why strategic managers should be involved in security policy decisions.

(d)   Methods of enforcing security policies.

Quality of written communication will be assessed in this question.   *(20 marks)*

Section 5: Developing ICT solutions

1   The development of a new management information system for an organisation can succeed or fail depending on various factors.

Describe three factors that would be important in making a success of the development, stating why they are important.   *(6 marks)*

AQA, 2008

2   A software house sells an Operating System (OS) for PCs.

(a)   Although alpha and beta tested before release to the general public, the OS sometimes fails to function correctly.

Give three reasons why this may happen.   *(3 marks)*

(b)   From time to time during the life of the OS, the software house distributes maintenance releases.

Describe two reasons why the maintenance releases may be necessary.   *(4 marks)*

AQA, 2006

Section 6: Systems developing tools and techniques

Based on case study on p117

1   (a)   Each media clip that Fxontap creates will need its own record in the new database.

(i)   Draw an entity attribute diagram to show the attributes that will need to be stored about each clip.   *(4 marks)*

(b)   The media clips will then need to be linked to the various projects that Fxontap are going to use them in. Some clips will be used in more than one project and most projects will use many clips. This is therefore a many to many relationship.

(i)   Why is a many to many relationship between entities a problem?   *(2 marks)*

(ii)   Suggest another entity that could be introduced to the system to solve the problem, and draw the new relationship diagram.   *(4 marks)*

2   The designers and other staff use a variety of platforms and often work outside the office. Discuss the impact this will have on testing the new system.   *(8 marks)*

Section 7: Introducing large scale systems

1   List four topics that should be included in an organisation's backup strategy.   *(4 marks)*
AQA, 2007

2   New software should be thoroughly tested.
    (a)   Describe what is meant by alpha and beta testing.   *(4 marks)*
    (b)   Explain two reasons why the new software may fail to operate correctly, even if the developer has followed an extensive testing programme.   *(4 marks)*
AQA, 2006

Section 8: Training and supporting users

1   A software house has produced a specialist package for the insurance industry.
    (a)   Name and describe three methods, which the software house could offer, of providing training for the users of this package.   *(6 marks)*
    (b)   Give three methods, which the software house could offer, of providing support for the users of this package.   *(3 marks)*
AQA, 2007

2   A part-time worker for an insurance company wishes to improve her job prospects. She has always been interested in the more technical aspects of ICT, and would like to learn more about network management.
    Discuss some of the training options that might be available to her and the benefits and limitations in her situation.   *(12 marks)*
New question

Section 9: External and internal resources

1   There are a number of different ways by which an organisation may obtain a software solution.
    Explain **one** benefit to an organisation of:
    (a)   purchasing an 'off-the-shelf' package   *(2 marks)*
    (b)   leasing software under a licence   *(2 marks)*
    (c)   using an in-house development team to create a bespoke solution   *(2 marks)*
    (d)   using an external software house to create a bespoke solution.   *(2 marks)*
AQA, 2006

2   (a)   An Internet service provider is considering offshoring its technical support facilities.
      (i)   Explain the difference between offshoring and outsourcing.   *(2 marks)*
    (b)   Discuss the benefits and limitations of offshoring this service for:
      (i)   the company and
      (ii)   its customers.   *(8 marks)*
New question

Section 10: Future developments

1 New developments in ICT technologies may bring great benefits to individuals and societies, but they may also bring with them moral and ethical dilemmas. Discuss your own research into ICT developments, including:

    (a)   Benefits that new developments may bring to individual people.

    (b)   Benefits that new developments may bring to businesses.

    (c)   Ethical and moral issues that may be associated with the technologies you have researched. *(20 marks)*

The quality of written communication will be assessed in your answer.

2 Based on case study on p117

Fxontap are an example of a business that needs to keep up with technological developments in ICT.

    (a)   What are the implications of this on the way the business is run? *(4 marks)*

    (b)   What are the potential consequences if they fail to keep up? *(2 marks)*

Practical issues involved in the use of ICT in the digital world

Introduction

This module gives you the opportunity to get involved in a real or realistic situation where you can use your skills, knowledge and understanding of ICT to solve a problem for a client. There are a wide range of projects you could get involved in e.g. devising a backup strategy for a local company or devising a plan for the managing the changeover from one software package to another.

Whatever you get involved in the chapters in this book will guide you through the steps needed to complete your solution successfully and how to meet the marking criteria set out for this unit.

Section 11: Getting started

It is worth remembering that your work for this unit will be judged from the standard of your project report and so it is vital that the report includes everything it needs to and that it is written to a high standard. This chapter gives you advice on what needs to be included and suggests tools you might use to make the process as efficient and painless as possible.

Section 12: Background investigation and analysis

This section will guide you through the process of identifying a client and identifying a project that satisfies a business need. You will need to provide a full introduction to your client and organisation and explain the current situation or the problem the client has. You need to present a business case for why the new system is needed based on interviews or other investigations. The first part of this section should end with you being able to produce a list of client requirements.

In undertaking thorough analysis, you will establish exactly what needs to be produced and how it will fit the needs of your client and/or users. At this point you will need to decide how you will judge how successful your final solution is by establishing evaluation criteria against which you can measure it.

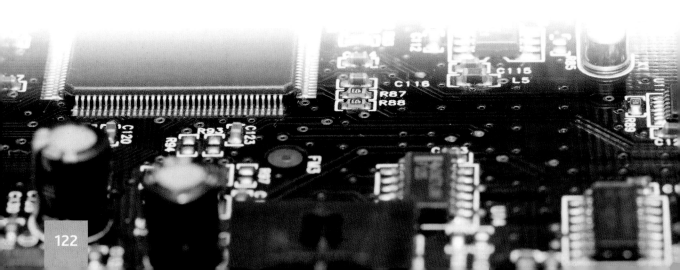

Section 13: Design and planning for implementation

This section will show you how to break the project down into tasks and plan how and when you will complete them. You need to think about the various ways that you could tackle the problem and produce what you feel are the most suitable designs, discussing them with your client so that you can be sure they approve of the solution you are proposing. A detailed test strategy and plan will be developed, which you will later use to test your solution. Your client or users will need to be trained to use your solution, and so you will need to plan this too.

Section 14: Documenting and testing your solution

This part of the report is where you will provide evidence that you have produced a working and effective solution. You will test your solution, correcting errors and making improvements until you feel it is ready to show your client, who will then need to carry out user acceptance testing and confirm they are satisfied with what you have produced. The documentation you will need to produce will vary, but might involve technical documentation and user training material.

Section 15: Evaluating the solution

This section really falls into two parts, evaluating the solution and evaluating your own performance. The first section helps you look again at the evaluation criteria you set early in the project and explain how close your solution came to fulfilling them. It should outline its strengths and weaknesses as well as suggesting ways in which it could be developed further.

The second section involves looking at your own performance and your own strengths and weaknesses, explaining how you would use that knowledge to improve your performance on future projects that you will undertake.

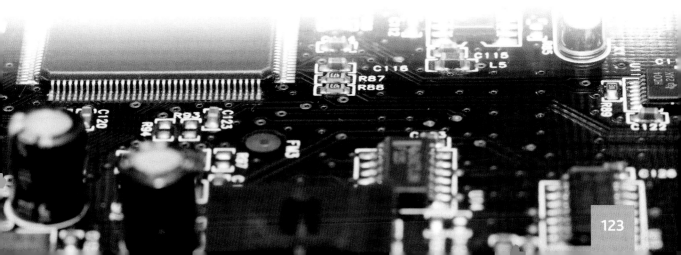

Specification	Topic content	Book chapter
Background and investigation	An introduction to the organisation A description of the current system (or existing situation) and its environment Identification of client and users A business case (reasons) for change Evidence of the use of relevant investigation techniques The requirements of the client	12 12 12 12 12 12
Analysis and deliverables	Statement of scope Description of the proposed system Documentation of processes Description of the users of the proposed system Evaluation criteria Agreed deliverables Evidence of checking the findings with the client	12 12 12 12 12 12 12
Design and planning for implementation 1	Evidence of investigating alternative design solutions Draft design work Final design work Plan for implementation, testing and installment, including proposed time scales Training requirements for the new system Testing strategy Test plan	13 13 13 13 13 13 13
Testing and documentation of the implementation	Evidence of testing including client and/or user testing Comprehensive documentation of the solution that would allow the solution to be used/maintained or developed further and is appropriate for the client/users	14 14 14
Evaluation of the implemented solution	A critical evaluation of the solution that would allow the solution to be used/ maintained or developed further which is appropriate for the client/user An evaluation of the student's own performance	15 15
The project report	The complete work should be submitted in the format of a project report	11

Getting started

In this section you will cover:

- the importance of writing style in your project report
- tools that can help make your report more accessible for its audience
- presentation of information
- tips and guidance on the content that should be part of your project.

11.1 The project report

The quality of your written communication skills and the ability to present documentation in an appropriate format are assessed separately as part of the coursework. The project should be well-structured, using suitable specialist vocabulary where appropriate and produced to a high standard. Consider your use of language and terminology carefully and use illustrations, including screenshots and diagrams wherever applicable.

The marking grid on the AQA website at (www.aqa.org.uk/qual/gce/ict_new.php) should be your guide as to your project structure and content and you should refer to it frequently to ensure that you are covering everything in sufficient depth.

Writing style

1 Always remember who you are writing for. For example, a maintenance guide may be for a user, the requirements specification will be for your client, while this report is for assessment and so is likely to be read by a moderator.

2 Use no more words than are necessary to express what you mean. You are wasting your own and your reader's time if you use too many words. While it may sometimes be satisfying to have written two pages of A4 on a topic, always consider whether it was all relevant? Most technical writing demands that you make your point as concisely as possible.

3 You are intimately familiar with the work, but your reader is not. You must continually re-examine your drafts with the critical eye of a potential reader. A useful technique here is to use a 'critical friend'. This is someone who can take the time to read your work and point out issues such as incompleteness or lack of clarity in your text.

Numbering

Use a consistent numbering style. The advantage lies in helping readers keep track of where they are within the report, especially if you help them by using indentations in your contents list. This is shown here.

1. Heading
   1.1 Subdivision
   1.2 Another subdivision
      1.2.1 Subsections
      1.2.2 Subsections
   1.3 And another subdivision
2. Second Heading

Presentation

Pages should always be numbered and you need to have a contents list at the front of the report. An index may also be appropriate in some documents.

Did you know?

Most word processors have spelling and grammar checking, which can include a check on your writing style. In addition, they often have readability statistics. Two common statistical values are the Flesch Reading Ease score and the Flesch-Kincaid Grade Level.

The Flesch-Kincaid Grade Level formula converts the Reading Ease Score to a US grade-school level. The score for this chapter is 9.7, which means that it should be accessible for a 9th/10th grader.

The output of the Flesch Reading Ease formula is a number from 0 to 100, with a higher score indicating easier reading. A Flesch score of 60 is classified as Plain English and this chapter scores 54.8!

To access this tool in Word type Flesch Reading Ease into Word's help seach engine.

For your project report it is wise to include your name, centre number and candidate number in the header or footer but your school or college should help you with that.

Diagrams and illustrations should be present throughout your report and these diagrams must be clear and large enough to be legible. A small, cropped image that is unreadable will not gain you any credit. All illustrations should be titled and have a reference number, i.e. Figure 2, so that they can be referred to accurately from within your written text.

Within the project report there will be documents relating to the deliverables, for example, a user guide. These documents should have their own table of contents and page numbering and be free from errors, including spelling.

Bibliography

There will be references in your work to other people's work and you should acknowledge this in a bibliography. You may need to show references to a range of sources, including books and websites, so here are some ideas as to how to set a bibliography out.

Books

Author's surname, first name, title of book (place of publication: publisher, year of publication):

e.g. McNee, Stuart and Spencer, Diane, *AQA Information and Communication Technology AS* (UK: Nelson Thornes, 2008).

Articles in a magazine

Author's surname, first name, 'title of article', title of magazine, volume (year), pages:

e.g., Allen, Lily, 'Identity: Computerized techniques', *Auto Computer ID*, 31 (2006), pages 437–441.

Electronic resources

Website

Author's surname, first name, name of page <URL> [date last updated]:

e.g. Catherine, Hazel, Guide to HTML <http://www.hc.co.uk/guides/writinghtml.html> [accessed 15 November 2007].

Article in an online encyclopedia

'Title of article', in title of encyclopedia, <URL> [accessed date of access]:

e.g. 'ICT Developments', in Encarta Encyclopedia, <http://encarta.msn.com> [7 June 2007].

CD-ROM

Title of CD-ROM (place of publication: publisher, year of publication) [on CD-ROM]:

e.g. Encarta 2004 Reference Library (UK: Microsoft, 2003) [on CD-ROM].

General tips

- Back up your documents on a regular basis. There should be at least one more copy that is separate to the main document store (i.e. not on the same disk!) e.g. on a CD-RW or flash drive. Every year, there will be at least one student trying to reproduce lost work or asking for the loss to be taken into consideration. As an ICT student you should know better!

▓ Track the date of documents. Version control is a professional skill. One idea is to keep the date in the header and change it manually when changes are made. Another is to use a version number in the filename and change this manually each time you save the work.

▓ Act on any feedback as soon as possible. Don't have old printed versions of documents still with corrections/changes written on them. Make those changes, back up and get rid!

▓ Keep any source documents and comments from clients/users together in a folder/binder. Date them and scan them in where appropriate. You can then include them in your work and also have the originals as a backup.

Project overview

As you work through your project, you will need to go through the following stages:

Background and investigation

▓ Investigate a problem supplied by your client.

Analysis and deliverables

▓ Analyse the client's needs and specify the requirements of a solution along with criteria that will later let you check if your solution is acceptable.

Design and planning for implementation

▓ Design your solution along with tests to check it against those criteria.

Testing and documentation for the implementation

▓ Implement your designs producing appropriate documentation, which may be technical or user documentation, or both, depending on your project.

▓ Carry out your test plans and so check whether you have satisfied the criteria and consequently provided what the client required.

▓ Carry out a series of acceptance tests, probably based on business scenarios, to prove your solution is acceptable to your client.

Evaluation of the implemented solution

▓ Evaluate the success of your solution using the criteria set at the start and evaluate your own performance across the range of activities that went into completing this project.

As you develop your project you will see that the evaluation criteria appear over and over again. If you do not set evaluation criteria then you will find it difficult to gain high marks for your work.

Remember for an ICT-based solution, evaluation criteria may include:

▓ response times

▓ overall time to complete a business process

▓ throughput/capacity

▓ anticipated growth linked to performance

▓ levels of accuracy for calculations and when checking input data.

AQA **Examiner's tip**

Ensure that you have created all necessary documents, e.g. for the analysis, design work, the documentation about your solution and your evaluation.

For example, if you are developing a new system for your client to handle up to 20 invoices an hour and each invoice is to produce a legible receipt on which the calculations are 100 per cent accurate, then these criteria provide an aim for your designs. They tell you what you should be testing for and achieving these criteria will tell you when you are successful. In your evaluation you use them to discuss if you were successful. If your solution has not been entirely successful, your report will need to reflect on why not. If your solution was a success, just how successful was it?

In this section you have covered:

- how to produce a well-presented report
- general tips to keep in mind whilst you are completing your project
- what you should include in your project report.

12 Background, investigation and analysis

Key terms

Business case: what the organisation wants to be able to do. Examples can include improving efficiency or providing a better quality service for the customer.

12.1 What is systems analysis?

The function of systems analysis is to:

- investigate and assimilate information about the way a system currently operates
- analyse the systems performance
- develop and evaluate ideas about how the system can be improved
- specify a new system that meets the requirements identified.

The aim is to produce a system that works effectively, efficiently and economically.

Project inception (or how to get off to a good start!)

How a project is set up in the first place is critical to its overall success. Bad practices followed at the beginning of a project have a habit of persisting and hampering development throughout the project.

The activities at this stage focus upon the definition of the **business case** and the project's objectives. The actual project cannot be developed until the client's requirements have been clearly defined. So, the initial work is all about confirming that the project proposal will meet those objectives.

In industry and commerce all the initial development work will be fully documented in a project feasibility report. Standard documents are normally used so that documentation adheres to common standards, enabling it to be understood by everyone. People concerned with the practice and management of systems analysis have always tried to develop and refine a standard approach to their work.

Documentation standards ensure that information is presented in a consistent form. This can speed up communication between the people involved, improve understanding of the functions and processes and make sure that all the necessary information is included. Overall it ensures that what you have done is recorded thoroughly and clearly enough for others to understand, which is why standards are used in all large organisations, public and private.

Activity

On your own, or with a partner, identify some standard techniques that exist, for example, SSADM. How many can you locate? Record your results in a table showing the name of the technique, who devised it, why they devised it and who uses it.

Section 6 of this book may give you a starting point.

Terms of reference

The work done during inception is based on the terms of reference. The terms of reference are originated by the client and define the scope (what has to be achieved), approach (who will take part in it, how and when it will be achieved) and the work to be done during the early stages of a project.

What would be contained in the terms of reference?

Title	Description
Background	An introduction to the project along with relevant background information to set the scene for the justification of this particular project. This will often include reference to the problems/errors that have occurred in the existing business system.
Aims and objectives of the project	State what the project sets out to do.
Deliverables	States what the project will deliver at each stage of the system lifecycle.
Scope	States what is within the scope of this project and what is not. It is also likely that any issues involved in attempting to put a limit on what this project is to cover will be highlighted now.
Resourcing	States what resources will be necessary and the time required from each person.
Timescales	Outlines the timescales and highlights any specific deadlines.
Reporting arrangements	Lists the initial reporting arrangements for the project.
Work plan	A detailed work plan needs to be drawn up.
Client and user	Description of who the client and users are and their roles in the system.

Key terms

Aims: a clear statement of intent signalling the purpose of the proposed project.

Objectives: more specific than the overall project aim. They set out what the project will do in specific, measurable terms. They should be realistic and achievable within the stated time frame.

 Coursework activity

Terms of reference

Get your client to agree to the terms of reference for your project. This should be a written/printed document, preferably on headed paper as it reflects that you have a real client!

The terms of reference will define what it is that the client believes they require of a completed system. This document will form the basis of your own 'project inception' work.

To make this task easier for your client, decide which of the above headings would be appropriate for your project and write a brief guide to give to your client that describes what you want them to do.

In addition you can begin to plan the project out within the timescales given to you.

12.2 Investigation techniques

There is a lot of information that you need to acquire from many sources and to do this you will need to use a variety of techniques. You also need to demonstrate the use of appropriate techniques in the Background and Investigation section of your project. For example, for a security policy project, techniques may include interviewing staff at all levels and document analysis.

These techniques have been covered in the AS book and in Sections 5 and 6, but to recap you could use the following:

- Interviewing
- Questionnaires
- Observation
- Thought showers
- Record searching/document analysis
- Fact recording

 Activity

Identify different documents you would expect to find in a large company and explain why they might be useful to you.

Stage 1: an introduction to the organisation

Once you have the terms of reference from your client you need to ensure that they are complete and accurate. Importantly you must also be sure that you know what is required and that you fully understand the scope of the project, i.e. what will be affected and what won't.

A common error at this stage is to confuse the problem and the symptoms! Consider a leisure club that hires out squash courts. In the system used to record bookings, customers' personal data is kept in one file and the actual booking details in another. Some customers have been charged the wrong amount. What is the problem? You could say that there are two files or that staff need more time so there would not be so many mistakes, but the main issue is that if customers are charged too much they are unlikely to return and may even tell others of the poor service. If unchecked, the problem will be the loss of custom!

 Coursework activity

Introduction to the organisation

Within your own project, write a full introduction to the organisation you will be creating a solution for. This must include background information about the organisation's environment e.g. its competitive situation and its relationship with its customers or suppliers.

 **Examiner's tip**

By completing this work you are starting to achieve row 1 of the mark scheme for Background and Investigation.

 Coursework activity

Creating a Problem Statement

Once you have your introduction to the organisation, you can extend this into a full Problem Statement for your project. The Problem Statement should extend the background of the organisation to include a background of the problem. Information should be given here that will help you to justify the need for an ICT solution, for example, the number of sales transactions that need to be recorded by the revised system. It is also important to consider the scope of your project, i.e. what aspects will be included in your project and what will be left out?

The Problem Statement must say what the problem is and how it arose. There may be business reasons, such as the need to improve efficiency. However if statements like this are used it is essential to know what needs to be improved and what the efficiency gains need to be. This will help you enormously when you evaluate the success of your project and will clarify for you what the client really wants. For example, 'The company currently has difficulties with late payments, which are causing cash flow problems. The existing payment collection system is manual and due to an increasing number of customers, staff do not have the time to check as often for non-payments and are unable to follow these problems up quickly enough to collect payment'.

📁 Coursework activity

Creating evidence for your project

One of the first steps as you begin your project is to set up a User Discussion Log. Completing a User Discussion Log as your project develops is important, providing evidence of interactions with clients and users. It would typically be presented in a table format with columns for the date, the name of the person you made contact with and their responsibility in the company e.g. sales manager.

Details listed should include the reason why you made contact and the outcome. For example, you may have met to clarify how the distribution manager allocates a delivery vehicle to an order. The log should summarise your discussion, as it is likely that any further level of detail will be part of your report, although you should provide the page reference of where to find it.

Stage 2: Organisational structure

When any organisation is set up, a structure of some sort is put in place. For any organisation to succeed there must be some form of structure present or there would be no systematic way of dealing with everyday issues. Without one, it would be hard to know who in the organisation has authority and responsibility for essential areas of the business.

So what do you need to know?

■ The structure of the organisation you are working for.

■ How decision making or responsibility is shared out.

■ How information is communicated in the structure … and why.

Understanding the basics of organisational structure is the starting point to understanding how information is passed around the company and who can make decisions based on it (look back to Section 1, Information, and Section 3, Management and strategies, for further information). The structure may be on three levels:

■ Strategic level: to define what information may be needed for senior management to make long-term decisions.

■ Tactical level: to discover what decisions are made at middle management level and what information is needed to make those decisions.

■ Operational level: to define the processes carried out to do the work and what information is created for management use.

📁 Coursework activity

Organisational structure

This will be particularly applicable for you if your project is based on a large organisation.

AQA Examiner's tip

Completing a User Discussion Log as your project develops is important and offers evidence to show interaction with clients and users.

AQA Examiner's tip

If you are undertaking a security policy project for a large company, for example, considering the organisational structure will be important.

Model the organisational structure for the company your project is based on. Identify on that structure the staff that will interact with your system and explain how they do it. Remember to record any interactions you have with your organisation in the User Discussion Log as you go.

Document the organisational structure as an appropriate chart, for example see Fig. 12.2.1, and identify the flow of information as well as those employees who will have an impact on your project.

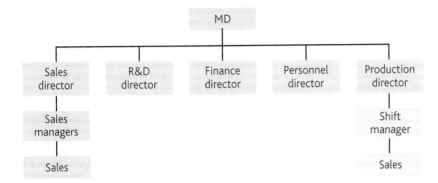

Fig. 12.2.1 *Example of an organisational chart*

 Coursework activity

Identifying users

Explain the role of each identified employee, e.g. the Sales Manager is responsible for making contact with customers and obtaining orders from those contacts.

Identify how each person is likely to affect this project, including detailing the skills they have to make the project workable. Focus on groups of users and not individuals, e.g. operators, and state which processes they use to do what job. This is also true for skills e.g. people will individually have different skills but to be able to complete a particular job, like a checkout operator, certain skills will be needed. For a quick overview it could be documented in a matrix. Remember to include any non-business users of the system.

Stage 3: identification of client needs

You need to provide a full description of the activity that is being investigated and the environment that it operates in. One reliable method of achieving this is to go back to the client's business requirements to confirm with the client that your understanding of those requirements is complete and correct. These will form the foundation upon which a new system is to be built so all requirements must be recorded, along with their priority. Recording the priority of the requirements allows objective decision-making when finally defining what the scope will be.

You need to be aware of any limitations that might affect the client's needs being realised. These can be internal factors, for example the company may have a policy that determines what suppliers they might use and that they should only buy in from environmentally responsible sources. Alternatively there might be external factors, such as legislation, which might control what a company wishes to do. Less obviously, external partners may insist on certain standards being met that affect how the company does its business. An example of this might be that when data are transferred electronically, specific file formats must be used. Another example may be when documents are to be produced; a report layout may be part of the company's standard procedures for British Standards accreditation and if they are changed they will have to re-apply. The new report may therefore have to maintain the old layout.

Client requirements for an ICT-related health and safety guidelines project may include producing a hard copy of the guidelines then developing an online test to ensure employees have gained the required understanding of the importance of meeting the guidelines.

Remember

If you can't identify why any particular requirement is needed you could begin to question if this is really needed at all!

AQA Examiner's tip

Do not write out lots of theory here. It will not gain you credit unless you relate this work to **your** project.

Coursework activity

Requirements of client

Identify each of your client's requirements, giving a short description along with the reason why it is needed as well as any major limitations to achieving this need.

There should be several client needs so number each requirement and give each one a clear title. For each complete the following headings:

- Requirement description – what is it?
- Reason(s) for requirement – why is it needed? What does it do for the user?
- Limitations – give any constraints imposed on the resolution of the requirement.
- Typical constraints may be: hardware/software, legal constraints, policy constraints, system-related constraints, for example this project may have to interface to a particular existing system and external interface constraints, i.e. standards used by external entities, that the project may have to conform to.

💡 *Service level requirements*

This section is about further refining the client's needs by looking at the service level requirements. You will need to define the client's needs carefully using quantitative and qualitative indicators and so establish the performance requirements; these could include any time limits for the process or financial constraints that have to be adhered to. For example, a pizza delivery company may wish to improve its process of collecting orders but knowing that the company has a directive that this must never take more than three minutes helps you gain a better understanding of what is needed from a solution. Establishing these qualitative and quantitative criteria now will allow you to investigate how they could be achieved and will help you to create a full set of evaluation criteria to use as you progress through your project work.

Coursework activity

Evaluation criteria

Complete as many of the criteria as you can for each business requirement.

Some examples are:

- Performance requirements (e.g. overall time to complete a business process)
- Timing requirements (e.g. output deadlines)
- Archive requirements (e.g. retention period for data)

■ System availability requirements (e.g. required hours per day)

■ Failure measures (e.g. contingency procedures. What happens if you computerise the pizza take-away service and you lose the ability to take orders using your computer systems? You will need a contingency plan other than just shut the shop until tomorrow!)

■ System integrity (e.g. error management).

■ **Remember**

It is unlikely that all of these criteria will fit every business requirement so if they don't apply don't use them!

◊ Stage 4: risk assessment

At this stage it is important to carry out an operational risk assessment. It is critical that you understand everything that could go wrong so you can develop a plan in case it does.

The objectives are to:

■ Identify risks to the confidentiality, integrity or availability of a system/business process and the data it uses.

■ Consider possible solutions that either reduce the risk of issues occurring or minimise the impact.

■ Identify potential solutions that could be used, either to reduce the likelihood of an issue occurring, or to minimise the impact if it does happen.

For example, in a backup system a specific risk is that the tape used for the backup is corrupted and when you try to restore the data it fails. It may be that there is a sequence of backup tapes for each day but the loss of one whole day's work may cost a significant amount of money to re-input. There may also be losses if the system cannot be used for its purpose until the data is brought up to date.

This work should enable the client and users to make informed decisions on necessary control requirements.

■ **Activity**

Imagine you are setting up a small business that hires out vehicles and drivers for special occasions such as limousines for school proms or weddings. You intend to use a computerised booking system. What risks are there and how would your business be affected? Try drawing them out as a spider diagram or mindmap.

 Coursework activity

Risk assessment

This may be useful for you if your project is, for example, a security policy.

Complete the risk assessment element of your project. You should be able identify the main threats to company assets and at least identify the impact to the company if those threats were realised, e.g. personal data held on laptops that are at risk of theft and the consequences of a loss of that personal data.

◊ Stage 5: current system – overview

It is unlikely that an effective solution can be produced unless the designer really understands what needs to be done. If your project was about payroll then you would need to understand exactly how to calculate someone's wage, including income tax and national insurance, which is a complex set of calculations. Equally if your client wants a new process that does not already exist then you must try to understand exactly what they want it to do. For example your client may want a digital signage system to give out information in their building to customers and staff. If they have never had one before you will have to understand what they want displayed and how frequently it will be updated.

Many solutions will encompass a lot of the original system with plans to alter certain parts of those existing systems. You need to start with an understanding of the existing system. To explain it all in one go would be very hard and error prone so analysis is all about taking small steps where each step can be used to check on the last and so ensure that nothing is missed.

An important tool at this stage is a data flow diagram. The purpose of an overview is to identify and examine the interfaces between the **external entities** and the system and this is just what a data flow diagram will achieve for you (see Section 6 for more on data flow diagrams).

Initially you are only representing the system at a high level of detail showing all the external entities and the information passing in and out of your system. Once the overview is complete then you can check the accuracy of your work with your user(s) before continuing to the next stage.

■ **Key terms**

External entity: someone outside of your system who puts data in, e.g. a customer buying goods, or someone who receives data or information from the system, i.e. a manager receiving a report.

■ **Remember**

When investigating existing systems, users are a part of this system. Consider their current roles and skill sets as part of your analysis.

■ **Key terms**

Process: a business activity, for example recording a customer's order.

🗁 **Coursework activity**

Existing system overview

For your own project, add a brief written description of the existing system (not the new parts).

Stage 6: description of current system and its environment

You now need to understand what happens inside the system. To do this you need to identify and analyse the **processes** that make up the system.

Modelling tools can help to identify the processes in the current system. Consider the following Level 0 data flow diagram:

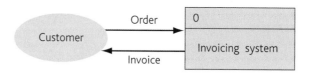

Fig. 12.2.2 *Level 0 data flow diagram*

This is used to identify the external entities and the way the data flows between them. Each data flow into the system will be handled by a process and all of the outputs will have to have been produced by a process.

The Level 0 can now be expanded to show the processes inside the system. A process such as taking a customer order will store some data, and this will be inside the system so a Level 1 diagram is needed to show what files or stores of data exist.

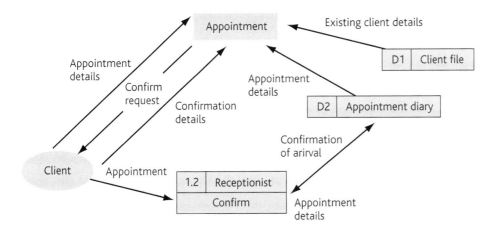

Fig. 12.2.3 *A level 1 diagram showing a customer making an appointment*

This Level 1 diagram shows a customer making an appointment. The appointment details are logged by the receptionist who also refers to them when the customer arrives for their appointment.

Referring back to the Oaktree school case study in Section 6, the following information flow diagram may be used for a security policy project.

To design a process for a system that creates an invoice you would need to know what information will be printed on that invoice and how that information is calculated from the data in the system. To design a process for a system that automatically re-orders stock you have to understand how that decision is made. The user knows the answers to these questions and you will need to use a range of investigation techniques to obtain the necessary information.

So what do you need to know for each process? Essentially you are defining **who** does **what**, **when**, **how** and **why**. You will also need to consider the current skills your users have and what their training needs might be. This will be particularly applicable if your project is a training programme. You can express this more technically, using the headings below.

Availability requirements

When should a process be available for the user? In a shop this could be the opening hours of that store. This could affect when backups of the data can be performed.

Inputs

What data items are input for this process and who inputs them?

- You may need to describe where they come from and how they are collected.
- If they are from a telephone conversation you will need to note the order they are collected in as you may need to replicate this in your solution.
- How are they verified or validated?
- What checks are made (or would the user would like to have made) to ensure that the data are accurate?

If collecting a membership ID, for example, you may need to look up that ID in a list. In addition you might have to obtain another data item to verify that the person is the ID holder, e.g. ask for their postcode or the answer to a security question.

Outputs

This is the required output information. You must be specific and state exactly what information will be needed. For example, if you plan to produce a receipt, exactly what information would appear on it?

Data accessed

Are there any data accessed in this process e.g. obtaining the credit limit details of a customer once their ID code has been collected?

Information or data stored/changed

Are any data changed in this process or new data added? Perhaps a copy of the invoice is filed away for later use or a customer's transaction is added to their balance?

Pre-conditions

These are actions or processes that must happen before this job can take place, e.g. a customer must have registered before they can hire goods.

Post-conditions

These are actions or processes that have to happen after this job has been completed, for instance updating a client's credit limit.

Frequencies

You need an idea of how often this process takes place. You usually cannot give a precise figure so a minimum, average and maximum is often given. The frequency with which a process takes place can affect a number of design issues. For example, there is a lot of difference between a process that occurs once a day and one that happens ten times every hour.

Process logic

This can be very important and it refers to the decisions that are made. Although decisions may be made by humans at present, in your solution rules may need to be set up to allow your system to make those decisions and you need to understand what they are. An example of this may be a decision on how much commission is charged depending on the value of a sale.

Data usage analysis

Your solution is likely to access files and you need to understand what types of access can occur (create, update, delete or read) for any data stores used in this process, for example, update a customer's balance and create a new record when a new person registers.

 Activity

Describe the processes for your project, as explained to you by your user, using the headings given above. List any areas where you need to obtain extra information from your user to complete the description.

Coursework activity

Proposed system

Add in the descriptions for each process of your project. At this point you should be describing your proposed system. This will involve using the analysis you have completed on the current systems and any revisions you are preparing.

Remember to use a numbering system (ideally this would tie up with your illustrations, for example your level 1 DFD if you drew one) and use a clear title for each process. Here's a reminder of the content:

■ Process name
■ Process owner (which of your users is responsible for this process?)
■ Definition (explain what this process does?)
■ Availability requirements (when does it need to be done)
■ Inputs (the data items input for this task and who inputs them, where they come from, how they are validated)
■ Outputs (the required output information)
■ Data accessed (data accessed in this process e.g. a check on the credit limit of a customer)
■ Data stored/changed (data changed in this process or new data added)
■ Pre-conditions (things that must happen before this job can take place)
■ Post-conditions (things that have to happen after this job is completed)
■ Frequencies (How often do things happen – Minimum, Average, Maximum)
■ Process logic (any rules that determine decisions made within the software. What rules/methods are applied to transform the data?)
■ Data usage analysis (this shows each access (create, update, delete or read) that may be made against the defined data stores).

 Coursework activity

Other considerations for the proposed system

Describe the system overview with your new processes included.

Remember to highlight what the differences will be if you are changing something and who this will affect. For example, what would changing e-mail package mean to those users who send and receive mail?

Provide an overview of the solution and the tasks involved, using a suitable diagram to illustrate the data flows. Where the tasks are the same, use the same numbering system as used in the analysis section of your project.

■ **Remember**

Even if your proposed new system does the same job as current system it won't operate in the same way and you must make the differences clear.

Changes and additions to user profiles

While some users will retain their roles, others will change and some new roles may be created. Analysis of this should include any external users of the system. You must also give details of any new skills your users will need to acquire.

Security and operational control issues

This would include the contingency procedures that are needed, backups/restores, disaster recovery procedures, restart/recovery procedures. You completed a risk analysis earlier and you must now make sure any important issues are made clear.

Technical implications

Now you know what the solution will involve can you foresee any technical limitations in providing the solution the user wants?

◪ Stage 7: data analysis

You need to identify the data that the proposed system will hold. The level of detail needed will depend on the type of project you are undertaking. A project investigating the changeover to a new word-processing package would need to consider all of the files used as these would need to be converted for use with the new software.

Data stores

Where appropriate you will need to describe each of the data stores. Explain what it is used for and any concerns e.g. what backup/restore issues are there? What archive issues are there? For the design of a training DVD for teachers on how to use a mark book, for example, data stores could include video files, spreadsheets, PDFs, web pages, etc.

You may need to complete a full analysis of the data stores before commencing the design process.

 Coursework activity

Defining data

Within your project, explain the data in your system. Summarise each data store identified in your system, for example, a level 1 Data Flow Diagram. In this case you would need to repeat for each and every data store.

Give each data store a clear name and use a numbering system. Where applicable link this to your data flow diagram. Include the following detail:

- Name
- Main purpose(s)
- Data items present
- Method of organisation including keys
- Backup/archive issues

Depending on your project it may be necessary to include an Entity Relationship diagram to show the relationship between the current data stores, and to complete a data dictionary for your system showing all data required.

◪ Stage 8: quantitative and qualitative evaluation criteria

At this stage, you have investigated in detail what the existing system does and how it does it and have carefully checked and documented what the user wants from the solution. You are now in a position to specify exactly what should be done to solve the problem posed at the beginning.

You must include specific evaluation criteria (measurable where possible) against which you will evaluate the success of your solution at the end of the project.

It is worth reflecting that inadequate analysis is a major contributor to the failure of newly introduced systems and only after all of the factors above have thoroughly explored should the design phase begin.

Coursework activity

Completing the evaluation criteria

You can now finalise the evaluation criteria you have been working on for your project.

Case study: Airbus A380 suffers from incompatible software issues 2006

The Airbus issue of 2006 highlighted a problem many companies can have managing projects. The problem was to do with the software used to design one of the world's largest aircraft, the Airbus A380.

The problem arose with communications between two organisations a French aviation company and a Hamburg factory who both producing important parts of the new aircraft.

The Germans and the French turned out to be using different versions of the software. So, when Airbus brought together the two parts of the aircraft the wiring on one failed to match the wiring in the other. The cables could not meet up without being changed.

While the problem was of course fixed, it cost considerable sums of money and set the project back more than a year.

☑ *In this section you have covered:*

- agreeing the project with a client
- how to describe the organisation and the users involved in your project
- how to describe the current system and specify what should happen in the new system
- how to define clients' needs and to understand the constraints on achieving those needs
- the deliverables of a system and how to specify appropriate evaluation criteria for that solution.

13 Design and planning for implementation

The biggest task for a designer is to teach others to understand their view of the solution and to put it into a form that others can share.

This is achieved through documentation, which includes anything that describes the system. At the design phase it is about providing plans that can be followed to build the solution, to check if the build has been completed successfully through different levels of testing and to plan for installing and changing over to the new system.

The documentation you need for your project will depend on the system you are planning to build. For example, a stock control system will certainly need a database design and technical and testing documentation, but a backup solution for a company may need operations, user reference and training documentation.

13.1 System design

There are two phases to design:

- Logical systems design – explains how the solution will work but excludes considering any hardware or software restrictions.
- Physical systems design – considers the alternative ways in which you can achieve the desired solution and specifies exactly what will be built with the specific hardware and software selected. For example, this could be designing a macro to automate a process using a spreadsheet or setting up a database using SQL.

Logical systems design

Logical systems design defines the systems procedures so that they can be agreed with the client before the physical design of the system begins. It is achieved by defining the interfaces, outputs and processing activities that will take place.

The purpose here is to show the overall structure of the proposed system in terms of what functionality it will deliver and to not be limited by technical issues.

For example, if you were designing a backup strategy for a company, the logical design will consider:

- what will be backed up
- when backups should happen
- (and possibly) how to recover the data, if lost, within agreed time limits.

You will need to be aware of any technological restrictions, but selecting specific software and hardware will come once a decision has been made on what process is needed to solve the problem. If you decide a backup is needed once a week, for example, this will demand very different hardware and software to a solution that needs hourly backups and is in constant use.

A detailed design must begin by referring to the systems overview. From here, you can begin to explain your method of solution in sufficient detail that a third party could follow. The descriptions and level of detail needed will depend greatly on your project idea but there are four distinct elements that you may need to consider:

- user interface standards
- dialogue design
- screen-based interactions
- report design.

Attention to these factors will ensure that the work done at the next stage will include all the relevant issues and so ensure a successful design. It is also a good method of checking the consistency of the design against the requirements specification and to obtain formal confirmation that the design is acceptable from your client.

User interface standards

This is to ensure that the visible aspects of the system match the client's requirements in terms of:

- 'look and feel'
- consistency with existing interfaces.

Any existing interface standards need to be fully understood and followed in the implementation of this project.

This will involve acquiring copies of any existing user interfaces, which may include:

- copies of all current screens
- reports and letters
- researching any existing standards for user interfaces.

The objective is to re-use wherever possible, to achieve consistency in the appearance of user interfaces. It may be necessary not just to document the standards in use but, in exceptional cases, to update them. In this specific case you may need to consider dialogue design.

Dialogue design

The nature of the interface between the users and the system will need to be designed, i.e. what data will need to be input and what information will be output. For example, if you were designing a training course that used an online multiple-choice quiz to check progress, you may have to consider how the trainee will select their answers and how any feedback on their success will be given to them.

This will involve designing all interactions between the user and the system.

Screen-based interactions

There are three aspects that may need to be considered at this stage:

- existing screens that can be used without change
- existing screens that need some modifications
- new screens to be developed.

For each dialogue, whether existing, to be modified or new, you should provide an overview: screens and/or windows to be used and what will flow between them, e.g. in a quiz each question might be marked individually but the running score is carried over to the next screen. This work may be represented diagrammatically as a **dialogue flow diagram**.

> ### Key terms
>
> **Dialogue flow diagram:** a set of logical steps expressed graphically that show how the user will pass through a series of dialogues to complete a task. Each dialogue either asks the user a question, gives the user information or confirms previously gathered data.

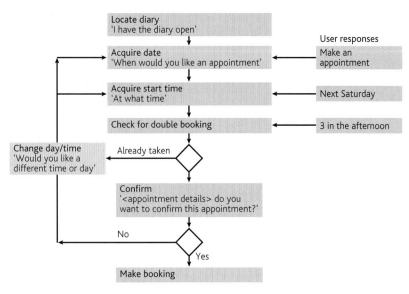

Fig. 13.1.1 *A dialogue flow diagram*

1 If there are existing screens to be used, without any changes, then simply provide a cross-reference to where these screens are used and to any further explanatory documentation.

2 New screens, as well as any existing screens that need to be modified, should be specified in terms of any templates to be used or re-used. The position and characteristics of everything that appears on the screen (e.g. literals, fields, buttons, icons) should be given, especially highlighting any modifications that need to be made to existing screens. If data is to be collected then field definitions should be provided in terms of length, type (e.g. numeric) and validation rules. A good example is the setting up of a template in a word-processing package where the operator will enter data at set points.

3 Input methods should be specified in terms of keyboard use, function key usage and the mouse. For example, in the word-processing template above, a macro could be assigned to a function key like F12 to autosave the document and print two copies automatically.

4 Explain what situations require error messages and what their content should be.

5 Document the use of any non-standard ways in which the users may supply input to, or obtain output from the system. This will cover any devices over and above the keyboard or mouse. Exactly what has to be documented will depend on the device, but examples of special I/O devices might include OCR, voice recognition or bar code readers.

Activity

Create a dialogue flow diagram for the following problem.

A catalogue company has a telephone-based ordering system. When customers ring they state the items they want, the delivery address and payment information. Items can only be purchased if they are in stock and there is no facility to reserve items when they do come into stock.

Report design

All outputs to be produced by the system must be designed carefully to ensure that they are fit for purpose.

Prototyping can be a valid approach here because if you are showing sample reports to users to get their feedback it is not worth producing a neat version of the report specification until the report design has been accepted – you will only have to change it!

For each report you need to specify the details about the report and its layout:

- Report name – what is it called?
- When is it produced and with what frequency?
- To whom is the report distributed and when do they receive it?
- What medium is used and is there a need for any special stationery or printing requirements?
- Volumes (average and maximum). How many are generated at one time?
- Who is the user of the report and what do they use it for?

Report layout

Here it will be necessary to visually describe the report in addition to documenting its content. For example:

- What fields will appear on the report?
- What will be their position, length and type (e.g. numeric)?
- From where is this information derived?
- What headers and footers will be needed and what will be their content?
- Will separator pages be needed?

Activity

Imagine a college produces a termly report on a student. The report has information on it from each tutor. Once collated it is printed onto A4 pages and sent (via post) to each student's parents or guardians. Each term this is done for 1400 students.

Design an appropriate report format for this document.

Documentation printing

Part, or all, of your project may be about producing documentation, e.g. a training manual or a company brochure. If a professional print company is producing the final product, you may need to consider:

- which pages need colour, and if that should be spot colour or full colour
- paper weight and finish
- binding method
- cover material
- formats supported (e.g. PDF)
- spacing issues such as margins and gutters.

The website of any online print house will provide an explanation of these terms and their impact on costings.

Coursework activity

Designing your solution

Begin work on the design element of your project, focusing on the following areas, where applicable:

- user interface standards

■ **Remember**

You should be consistent in your use of layout and colour so that the user is not confused by a bewildering collection of colours. Thought should also be given to how long the user will be using your system or the hard copy of any docuementation you produce, such as a security policy, i.e. avoid colour schemes that would strain your eyes over long periods. Use of graphics and colours can add great value to your work but only when used sensibly.

AQA Examiner's tip

Prototyping an interface is a sensible approach that will involve you in a dialogue with the client, and/or users until your designs are approved. Show them your designs and ask them to make add their comments to those designs, as this is the best evidence that they have seen your work and participated in the design process.

■ **Remember**

For each process consider who does what, when, how and why in order to describe the process.

■ dialogue design
■ screen-based interactions
■ report design.

Designs for a database management system should include all menus, forms and reports. Forms and reports can be individually drawn (by hand) in each task description, but adopting a standard style to which you always work will improve the usability of the finished implementation and make the work much quicker to complete!

Physical systems design

The aim is to create a system design from the detailed descriptions of the processes given so far. For your project, you have considered what needs to happen and now need to decide on what hardware and software you need to make it happen. It may be that the proposed logical design will need to be adjusted to allow for any physical constraints.

In the example of a backup system, we would conisder hardware and software requirements, i.e. you know how much data needs to be backed up and in what time period, so you can use this information to select the type of backup media and equipment. However, you may need to operate within the constraints of what your client already has, particularly if they do not have the budget to buy from new. Consequently you may now have to make compromises based on the limitations of the resources you have available.

The physical design may include considering the following elements:

■ alternative solutions
■ draft design
■ final design
■ test strategy and plan
■ training requirements
■ plan for implementation, testing and installation.

This stage will close with formal confirmation from the client/users that the design is acceptable, in that it is consistent with requirements specification given at the end of the analysis, and that all work has been done to ensure that the next stage of building the solution will be successful.

Alternative solutions

You need to consider a relevant range of possible ways of solving the problem. To do this, the methods available will depend greatly on the project you have chosen. For example if you were implementing an order invoicing system for your client then possible alternatives might include:

■ an off-the-shelf package
■ spreadsheet software
■ database management software
■ an improved manual system.

Alternatively, for the alternative methods of delivering a training course options could include:

■ paper-based manual led by tutor
■ online course, led by tutor with paper-based materials
■ online course, led by tutor with Internet-based support materials
■ online course, with remote support by tutor.

For a library system, a possible solution for consideration might be the use of a Database Management System (DBMS).

A DBMS allows the developer to implement customised forms that incorporate the use of Windows controls, such as combo boxes, list boxes and text boxes, to provide a graphical user interface. This interface could provide access to the user to perform the following tasks under macro control:

- entry of new members
- entry of new stock
- entry of loans
- logging returns
- query facilities (enable enquiries to be made such as non-return of loans)
- reporting facilities (allow overdue book lists and reminder letters to be produced).

In each case you must relate the possible solution to the requirements of your own project.

Reasons for choice

Having explored the alternative methods, you need to evaluate and detail how well each performs against your evaluation criteria, given in the requirements specification of your analysis. Problems can occur, though, when several methods are all capable of achieving your criteria so which one to select then?

In this case you need to decide which aspects of the possible solutions are most important in your situation. You may wish to consider:

- Export – can standard formats be created for export to other systems?
- Reporting – how easy is it to set up customised reports?
- Skills to operate – how easy will it be for staff to operate given their existing skill base?
- Overall cost – purchase, development and maintenance costs.
- Time of development – how quickly can the solution be available?

You will then need to decide how much each is worth in relation to the others. One way to deal with this is to use a total mark, e.g. 100, and allocate a value to each factor. The higher the value the more important it would be.

Now you can score each option out of that total. For example, in Fig. 13.1.2 the user has decided that the database management system has the best export options, although at 9 out of 10 they still do not match what is required perfectly. A user has also decided that while an improved manual system is possible, the reporting from it would still be very poor and has scored this as only 1 out of 15! This evaluation could be done by a range of interested parties and the scored averaged out.

You must justify all of the scores that you allocate, but at the end one should have the highest total and this becomes the preferred choice of solution. Finally, summarise why it is the best option and state that this will be your chosen way of developing the solution.

> **Did you know?**
>
> The website www.softwareevaluation.co.uk allows you to compare software packages for a purpose of your choice.

	Export	Reporting	Skills to Operate	Overall Cost	Time of Development	Total
Value	10	15	20	25	30	100
Off-the-shelf	5	5	15	11	14	50
Spreadsheet	6	4	10	10	5	35
Database	9	8	12	8	5	42
Improved manual	1	1	20	12	14	48

Fig. 13.1.2 *Evaluating possible solutions*

Coursework activity

Investigating alternative solutions

Within your own project, detail all relevant alternative solutions and how they would work, justifying which one you have chosen and why. Clearly state the reasons for your choice, including how effective it will be and any limitations you still expect. The criteria for selection need to be taken from your requirements specification.

Draft design

Design overview

This is an overview of how the business processes will actually work with the technology selected. This may involve explaining:

- What hardware needs to be used and why?
- Where that hardware will be located?
- What type of network structure (e.g. client/server) may be needed or how remote sites might be connected together for data transfer?
- What software is needed for application components (e.g. operating systems, DBMS, applications software, scripting tools, communications software, productivity tools)?

 Coursework activity

Design overview

Complete the design overview for your project's design.

Data design

If your solution stores data then at this stage you should consider how that data will be physically stored using the software and hardware available. For example, your online training package with multimedia facilities needs sets of questions to check user understanding and you need to store their answers to provide a detailed report for trainee and instructor at the end of the course.

For a file of data, exactly what needs to be written down will depend on the technical environment and the file type, but you will need to provide the file name, the storage medium, how it is organised and how it is accessed.

Additional issues that need to be considered regardless of what software you are using include:

- Protection requirements – read only, write only?
- Access authorities – who is allowed to do what with the file?
- Data volumes and space requirements. An estimate of the file store size may be needed. This is, of course, critical for any kind of backup system.
- Depending on the type of project, you may need to define the structure of the file. There are a range of techniques depending on your application, e.g. spreadsheet, but as a minimum you should provide the record types and for each record specify the fields and their descriptions. For example, part of your project may involve mail-merge facilities and you must know what fields exist to include them in any standard letters.
- For a solution based on a database managment system you will need to define its overall structure (usually a diagrammatic representation, illustrating tables and their relationships) and for each table the fields, keys and indexes.

In addition you should consider:

File clean-up procedures

Identify the automated and manual procedures that will ensure that the files are maintained at optimum operational size e.g. removing out-of-date data.

Backup, recovery and reorganisation strategy

If you have files then you must document the strategy to be followed to ensure that databases and files continue to perform efficiently and that, in the event of any failure, they can be recovered within the required time.

Data back-up

When will this be performed and with what frequency? What types of back-up (complete/incremental) will be taken on those occasions. How many copies will be taken, what media will be used and what are the storage arrangements (onsite/offsite) for those copies. Who will carry out the process and what are their roles?

Checkpointing

Is when a back-up is done and kept as a reference point, e.g. a school or college might do this at the end of each academic term.

Recovery requirements

Define what your client's data availability requirements are and so define the recovery timescales should failure occur.

 Coursework activity

Draft design work

Complete the Data Design for your project.

For each file you may need to provide the following details:
- file name
- storage medium
- organisation and access methods.

Additional issues which need to be considered regardless of what software you are using include:
- protection requirements
- access authorities
- data volumes and space requirements.

You will need to define the data present and this could include providing a record structure complete with field names and data types.

In addition you should consider:
- file clean-up procedures
- backup, recovery and reorganisation strategy
- data back-up
- checkpointing
- recovery requirements.

Process specification

You need to describe what each process in your solution must do in enough detail to allow a third party to create and test the process. Note that many parts of the process specification (e.g. file layouts) will already exist elsewhere and so should simply be referenced and not repeated. You have already explained what you want from the process so you are now explaining how the technology will be used to achieve what you want.

The following would apply to most of the processes in your solution:

1 A summary, which should include a short name (what everyone will know it as). Give a brief overview of how it will work and detail the software and hardware needed for this process. Be precise, including giving software version numbers as different versions may work differently or have different facilities. Some software may also need specific hardware to work properly.

2 Details of all inputs. This would obviously include data input from the user or from files but may also include links with other software and special input devices. For example, if one of your tasks was to produce a leaflet containing a price list, this price list might exist in a spreadsheet and you should plan to link to it dynamically.

3 Interactions with and changes to the current system. You may refer to items already designed e.g. interfaces, screen formats, report layouts and error messages, but you may have to include technical details that are now needed because of the software selected. For example, in an HTTP solution output may be needed to a cookie to be read from later, perhaps for personalisation.

4 Full description of how the process will be done with the hardware and software selected. You have already said what you want the process to do but now must explain how those things will actually be done within the technology you have selected. For example, one objective in your project may be to do data analysis for decision making. You will have already decided what information is needed and how it should be presented but may now decide that the best solution involves a spreadsheet with a pivot table – here you would show what is needed to set up that pivot table.

5 Restart and recovery requirements. What happens if this component fails and what would you have to do to get it back working again? What are the security issues; how do you protect from accidental or deliberate misuse of this process?

6 Testing requirements. Are there any special testing considerations, that need to be included later in the testing phase? Existing procedures that are subject to change may need regression testing.

Final design

 Coursework activity

Finalising your design

Once you have a design that your client is happy with, you have achieved a final design. Write up any amendments, ensuring that you have fully documented revisions and feedback that have influenced your design as you worked through your draft design stage.

Test strategy

A test strategy is an overall plan for all testing activities that will be carried out to check that the original needs have been met. Testing is a set of practical activities that can be planned in advance and conducted systematically.

While functions like validation or system navigation will need to be checked, the test strategy is concerned with checking the solution as a whole. If, for example, you said in your evaluation criteria that a report should be

 Coursework activity

Draft design work

Complete the Process Specification for your project's design .This involves considering the six areas outlined above for each process in your solution.

 **Coursework activity**

Checking your design with the client

Collate and complete your draft design and share this with your client. Following this stage, it may be necessary to make amendments to your initial draft. This may be an iterative process.

AQA **Examiner's tip**

It is critical that you obtain evidence of your client's feedback and revise your design accordingly.

produced in two minutes, be 100 per cent accurate and be appropriate to the user's needs then this is what the testing should be aimed at proving.

Who will be involved in the testing process? Allowing the creator of the system to exclusively test what they have built can cause conflict, especially when testing shows the solution isn't correct! Organisations may set up an independent testing review panel.

You may need to identify:

- Build manager: This person would be responsible for build testing, which are checks that take place as the solution is being built or developed. In this project it will be you!
- Users involved in testing: Which users of the proposed solution will need to be involved as the solution is tested?
- System testing team leader.
- User testing team leader.

In large scale organisations you would need to identify testing review panel team members. The testing review panel would monitor both system testing and user testing. They will be responsible for tracking and the control of any errors located. They would also decide on any regression testing policy that might be needed.

You will need to create an outline testing schedule to identify key timescales and milestones with known important dates, including when the testing is to be completed. This would be as part of your plan for implementation, testing and installation.

So what is in a test strategy?

The strategy itself requires you to identify and define appropriate levels of testing.

For each level, you should describe:

- The purpose and scope of the test and what deliverables are expected.
- Who will take overall responsibility (i.e. the team leader for this level)?
- What major activities will take place and which people will be involved?
- What techniques and types of tools will be used?
- What resources are needed, including source documents for any test conditions.

The following list recaps the possible testing levels you may need to engage in, detailed in Section 5.

- module/unit tests
- integration tests
- functional tests
- systems tests
- user tests
- operational tests.

Test plans

Test plans are a technique for recording the tests to be carried out and the expected results of the tests. Typically a plan includes a test number, the type of test, what is being tested, what test data will be used and what results are expected. The actual results will be documented in the testing phase.

The plan can be divided up into the various test types, for example unit testing, system testing, etc.

Remember

Your client and users will also be involved in the testing process.

AQA Examiner's tip

Evidence of functional or unit testing is not required as part of your project report, although these tests are still necessary and you will need to complete them within the implementation, testing and installation phase of your project.

■ Case study

This test assesses a client requirement that data is recorded with 100 per cent accuracy and no data loss. During implementation the input data has been validated and tested to ensure only valid members can hire equipment, which is available for loan.

A membership number is always five digits and an equipment ID is always five characaters in the format letter, letter, digit, digit, digit. The following members exist 00234, 00456, 00987, 11090 and 12345. The following equipment IDs exist SW567, TS001, TS002, VW444 and XY567. No equipment is on loan at the start.

Test No.	Test data	Reason	Expected outcome
001	Membership No: 00234 Equipment ID: SW567	Test with an existing member and an available piece of equipment	Loan is recorded
002	Membership No: 00987 Equipment ID: SW567	An existing member but the piece of equipment is now on loan and this transaction should not be allowed.	No data stored. Message box with 'Transaction refused' displayed.

Coursework activity

Creating your test strategy and plans

Complete the test strategy and necessary test plans for your project using your client requirements and qualitative and quantitative evaluation criteria. You need to think carefully about exactly what headings your test plans will need, based on the type of tests you are intending to run.

Training requirements

You must identify the training implications of the proposed system. For a reminder on the types and methods of training available, see Section 8.

■ Activity

Referring back to Section 8 if necessary, complete this activity:

■ You are asked to advise an organisation on the introduction of a new software package.

■ With the aid of three examples, explain why different users may require different levels of training.

■ Following the initial training you advise subsequent training for users. Give two reasons why the organisation may require this.

Coursework activity

Training users

Update your project with details on training users of your proposed system with reference to their existing skills and agreed deliverables.

Plan for implementation, testing and installation

Planning for conversion

At some point the new system will have to come into use. If your project has been about preparing employees for a new version of a word-processing package, for example, then there comes the point when they must start to use the new package and stop using the old. It is important we plan for that change so that nothing goes wrong and we must first select how the changeover will be done.

Changeover

There following are methods which can be carried out to manage changeover:

- direct
- pilot
- phased
- parallel.

For more information on these changeover methodologies, please see Section 7.

File conversion

The conversion of existing files to a format suitable to the needs of the new system will need to be completed before any new system goes live. In the word-processing example, a business will have a whole variety of standard letters, probably set up as templates, that need converting but administrative workers use those templates to create working documents. In some cases the work may need to be re-entered at the keyboard but this is expensive, as it is labour intensive, and needs to be carefully controlled to avoid inaccuracies – both in the original and the new version.

If a college had a new management information system and the data had to be retyped how long would it take? If it took 10 minutes to enter one record and there were 1200 students, this would take 200 hours continuous work!

Usually some automated method of converting the data is needed. This could easily be a whole A level project on its own! Other problems you are likely to encounter include editing fields into a new data format and entering new data that was not used before e.g. what if a date of birth was needed but was not previously collected?

Additionally, accessibility of live files is always an issue. If they are in use, when is the best time to convert them? Closing the system down to change may seem simple but would it affect the business?

Case study: a dental practice

A dental practice is moving from a paper-based record system to a software system bought in from a software company who specialise in this type of software. What would be part of your changeover strategy for the practice. When would they transfer over their patient records so that they are available in the new system?

There are a number of factors that will need to be considered when planning including:

- How busy is the practice?

■ Are they sufficiently staffed to handle the increase in work during the changeover?

■ How many records need to be transferred to the new system?

There are a number of ways to approach the changeover phase:

■ Before beginning all old records should be purged i.e. records of deceased patients or patients who have moved. There is no point in copying over out-of-date data.

■ Taking a day-to-day approach, the office could convert and perform the data entry for every patient that will be seen the following day on the day before their appointment. One day is chosen for the 'go live' date and from that point forward all data is entered into the new system the day before the appointment. Over time each day's work becomes less and less as patients return for subsequent visits. This approach works well for companies that are well staffed or smaller in size.

■ Entering in patient dental charts weeks or months in advance can also be done. The challenge with taking this approach is that the data on the 'go live' date may be outdated from when the data was originally entered into the system weeks or months before. In most cases all the data will be input but at the time of the visit the data is updated by the staff and checked over by dentist during the appointment to double-check its accuracy.

■ Using a parallel changeover will allow the dental practitioners to ease into using a new system while removing staff dependency on the old system as patient data will be found in both the new system and the old paper record. While taking this approach causes extra work, it can help staff move to new systems more effectively. Implementing a parallel system could be done by continuing to have the dentist use the paper system for dental charts but all data from the appointment is entered directly into the new system thereby making the data accessible in two versions at all times.

■ Hiring the help of temporary employees to assist in the process of data entry of old information into the new system can be relatively inexpensive and can reduce the strain on existing employees.

 Coursework activity

Changeover plans

Start thinking through your changeover plans for your project.

■ How should you change and why?

■ What will this involve doing and who will do it?

■ What needs to be put in place before the change is actually made?

■ Will any data need converting?

■ Will any hardware need to be installed?

■ What about software?

 Coursework activity

Plan for implementation, testing and installation

Complete the plan for implementation, testing and installation for your project. This should include timescales and deadlines.

Last word

This is the end of the design and planning phase. At this stage you should now know:

- what you are going to create
- the hardware and software needed to do it
- importantly, that you have planned for the testing that will take place, as your main objective now is to create a system which is genuinely useable by the people who need it in their place of work.

You must understand the technical implications of the software you are using, as it may take many hours to overcome unforeseen problems. For you this may mean incomplete work by the time deadlines arrive, and commercially it could mean costs spiralling above the allocated budgets and penalties for not delivering the project on schedule.

Do people get it wrong commercially? The answer is yes!

Case study: Terminal 5 at Heathrow revisited

Do you remember the case study from Section 5, in which insufficient testing was blamed for the problems that occurred on the opening day of Heathrow's new £4.3 billion Terminal 5?

Well, the lack of training received by staff has also been cited as a contributing factor, in a report published by the Transport Select Committee in November 2008.

Fig. 13.1.3 *Baggage system at Terminal 5*

Before you start to implement your own solution research and identify why the baggage handling system really failed. Consider both testing and training – what happened to the plans for these as this new system was being implemented? Think about changeover; obviously this was a new system so it had to be an immediate changeover, so what implications does this raise for testing and training?

In this section you have covered:

- assessing and evaluating alternative solutions
- how to describe the design of a system
- how to plan for the conversion from the current system to a new system
- how to approach the testing of your solution and what to document
- planning training for those who operate and use your solution.

> ### Remember
>
> Remember that failure to plan is a plan for failure! You must be clear on what you are building and, therefore, whether you have created the solution your client desired.

Documenting and testing your solution

Having completed the analysis and design you are now ready to start creating your solution. The documentation you produce depends on your problem and the way that you choose to address it. For example, it could be a website using HTML, or a set of inter-related spreadsheets or even a customised database solution. In these cases technical documentation might be needed for someone to develop the solution further in the future, i.e. change it to do something new and user documentation could be needed to talk users through the changes to their working practices.

Alternatively you may have designed a training course for ICT staff, or a changeover plan for moving from one word-processing package to another. You may even have developed an implementation plan for introducing wireless networking into a company. These would all require different types of documentation. Understanding the different types and knowing which one to use and why, is what this chapter is all about.

You will also need to test how well it works. Although a wide range of testing techniques are available to you, your main objective is to complete enough appropriate tests to satisfactorily prove that the system you have created is a practical, useable solution to the client's problem.

14.1 Documentation

Who is going to produce the documentation? The answer here is you, of course, but what about a large company and are there any lessons you can learn from their approach?

What about those who developed the solution? Often they are too close to the system they developed to document it thoroughly. They tend to assume a high degree of technical knowledge, which users often do not possess. Another factor is that they are probably better employed doing what they are paid to do which is to develop new systems and maintain existing ones!

Documentation is usually better produced by a person not involved in development, either an employee of the company or an external resource. Such a person will specialise in the production of documentation and will, therefore, do a professional job. Their role is often described as a **technical writer or author**.

Types of documentation

What you produce depends on your solution. The following documentation types are examples of what may need to be produced, and you will need to agree with your client which documents are required for your system. No system you produce is likely to need all of them.

For example, if you have built a customised spreadsheet to fulfil your user's needs then you would need maintenance documentation and a user guide. You might need a procedure manual to explain how the software fits into the other processes within the company.

You will have already identified and agreed with your client what deliverables you will be producing. This could include:

Key terms

Documentation: any form of information that needs to be communicated about a system. It may be on paper but it could occur in many other styles and formats e.g. an online help system or a multi-media training guide.

Technical writer or author: a professional writer who puts technical information into a more easily understandable language for readers. The writer would prepare maintenance manuals and user guides for example, not just for computer based systems but all kinds of technical products – even toasters!

User guide

This is documentation designed for someone who will interact with an ICT-related system. It may be paper based, but can be online or electronic and is designed to guide the user through using an application. Commonly it will be based on the tasks the user needs to complete to do their job.

Technical or maintenance documentation

This is written for those people who later want to operate, modify or repair the solution you have created, so they can understand it enough to complete those tasks. Typically it would contain details on file structures including organisation and access methods. It would contain fully annotated listings of any code generated e.g. HTML, macros and the designs for that code or how the solution was set up e.g. which data and calculations were selected for a pivot table.

Training manual

Training manuals are documents designed to show the reader how to do something. They could take three main forms:

1 As an introduction prior to a training session.

2 Instructions and examples to be worked through during a training session.

3 As a reference after a training session is complete.

Broadly a training manual may contain a sequence of scenarios through which the reader can work. They would contain normal cases and when confidence builds, error conditions and unusual events. At one extreme, some will include detailed step-by-step instructions, and at the other just the exercises to work through with space for the reader to record their own actions, which they can refer to later if, needs be.

Training instructor's manual

This would contain all the materials which will be made available to the trainee but importantly should contain detailed plans for the training session. This will include timings for the sessions showing when the instructor will speak when trainees will work independently or in groups on completing tasks. Often a script is included which the instructor will follow. This ensures that the instructor does not have to rely on personnel experience and that all trainees always get the same experience.

If the course finishes by assessing trainees and issuing certificates then the test materials, a marking scheme and notes to explain how the work is marked and how to interpret the results will be included in the instructor's pack.

Installation guide

These are instructions needed by technical staff to install and configure the hardware and/or install the software on that hardware and then make it accessible to the user. Typically an installation guide might contain sections on:

- Installation planning: this would offer an overview of the process, highlight any additional products needed e.g. printer drivers, discuss any preparation work needed as well as possible restrictions i.e. compatibility.
- A detailed guide on installation itself and a section on post installation activities.

Normally there would be a checklist for the user to follow as well as a specification of all hardware and software components.

Procedure/operations manuals

These manuals will include information on:

How to complete daily operations. Importantly they show how the solution is used within the other processes in your client's organisation. e.g. developing a solution to scan school registers using OCR technology still has to fit in the registers being marked and returned by teachers and the data being stored so it can be integrated later.

Special operations e.g. special tasks that can be needed from system shut-down to annual data transfer.

Troubleshooting. In case of any problems this document should contain all information required by internal staff or external experts to appraise the problem.

Other tasks (e.g. Hardware/Software/License upgrades) required to keep the system running within the expected performance limits and prevent unplanned problems (e.g. because of a network application exceeding the software license limit).

Policy handbook

All organisations have policies that will be stored as part of a policy handbook. If your design means that changes need to be made to an existing policy, this would need to be documented and passed on to the person responsible.

Startup guides

As the name suggests this is a short guide to get the user started which would focus solely on the basic activities they need to complete. In some cases the guide would be presented in a way that it could be kept with the user or at their workstation as a quick reference.

14.2 Testing

Planning for testing should have been completed alongside your design work and you should have completed testing of the functional units in your solution as it was developed. This means that you have checked the individual components and they work as intended e.g. if a macro was written to make a copy of a template then you will now test it to make sure it does.

Although your solution should have passed its functional tests you now need to complete appropriate tests to show that your solution works together as a whole and is acceptable to your client and user.

For example, if one of the processes in your solution was to produce a training manual then while this may now be available in the format described e.g. a PDF file you now need to assess whether the manual is effective in training users to complete the tasks needed.

The purpose here is to show whether complete processes work according to the specification given and whether the system as a whole solves the problem given. If you promised a training course that could be delivered in five working hours to 12 staff and that at the end of that course they could carry out the software tasks they were trained for then did you deliver?

Testing evidence

You must prove that you have carried out appropriate testing. You will already have plans for testing your solution but there must be evidence that the testing was conducted. Hard copy evidence is always needed. This may be screen dumps to show what is happening or it may be printed output. If your solution is supposed to produce a printed receipt for a customer then you must print out a copy showing exactly what the customer will receive, it is not enough to show a screen dump of what it would look like in print preview mode, you must print it out.

Some tests are then easy to prove but if you created a training course for your project – how will you test that? The following sections will take you through the main types of testing you may need:

Documentation testing

Have you bought something, taken it home, got it out of the box and started to assemble it? Are you the sort of person who puts it together without the instructions or do you study them closely before making a start? I guess you know how frustrating it is when the instructions can't be followed and don't make any sense to you! All the documentation you produce needs to be tested because if the user cannot use it for the purpose it was intended for then the whole product is likely to be unused.

Testing documentation can be problematic as it is difficult to prove if a user manual is acceptable in the same way as proving whether your software can calculate VAT accurately or not.

1 Firstly, you yourself should check that all aspects are complete and have been produced as required. If you promised a quick start guide, detailed user guide and a quick reference guide, laminated as a double-sided A5 sheet, have you done it?

2 Next a company would use professional proofreaders to check for spelling and grammar errors and to see overall if the guide is readable by the intended audience. Due to the cost, you may have to use employees with strong written communication skills instead, but whoever does it will provide evidence by annotating the documentation to show any errors and mistakes and should present a written report summarising what they thought. This evidence should be added to your report.

3 If you have written a policy or a strategy then it may be necessary for external bodies to check your work. e.g. a professional body to check for compliance or legal specialists to ensure conformity with the law. You will need written feedback from your client if you create a policy that all employees will have to follow e.g. a security policy.

4 Finally you can trial documentation with people who are unfamiliar with the situation to see if they can follow all the documented procedures. If the testers can't successfully complete the procedures then clearly the documentation needs to be improved. You will need to document these tests and clearly indicate where there are errors or mistakes so that improvements can be identified.

If you follow these steps and review all the documentation thoroughly then you will reduce or remove a big obstacle to ensuring the users can operate your solution successfully.

Testing of training

Delivering a training course and all associated material may well be a deliverable of your project and consequently all aspects need to be tested before you deliver that course for the first time.

■ All documentation needs to be tested before you even consider how it would be used in the training session.

■ You or your instructor for the training session should go through the session at least once. You are checking: that the timings work, i.e. that there is enough time for you to talk through the script; that all materials are available e.g. a presentation is available when the training booklet calls for it; that all resources are available, e.g. what if each trainee needs a laptop computer?

Acceptance testing

Developers of solutions write unit tests to determine if the part of the solution they are working on is doing the right thing. Acceptance tests exist to determine if the system, as a whole, is doing the right things.

Acceptance tests represent the client's interests and give them the confidence to know that the solution has the required features and works as specified. In theory when all the acceptance tests pass, the project is done. In the end it is the client who owns the solution you have been developing and acceptance testing allows the client to ensure that the solution meets their business requirements.

A plan for acceptance testing must state the acceptance criteria. These should have been defined at the end of the analysis stage in the requirements specification where the deliverables of the project were decided. Before starting the acceptance test, you must be clear on what the criteria are that will be used to decide whether your system is acceptable or not and how that decision will be made.

e.g. it may have been decided that any standalone PC in the company could be restored for use, after failure, in 30 minutes once the hardware fault had been fixed but is any margin for error acceptable?

Remember that the customer may want to check some aspects thoroughly for themselves even though you feel that you have tested them yourself at earlier stages. For example, you may have tested response times and the robustness of your security, but your user still needs to satisfy themselves that your solution works to their satisfaction. Remember if your system doesn't do what users want, it is practically worthless.

You should produce a work plan for the tests where you define the activities which need to be carried out.

Ideally the client (or their representative) along with other involved members of the client's organization, will help to write the tests in a language business people understand, not in technical terms. Once written, the tests should ideally be carried out by a wide range of users, tracking those which have been carried out, recording if they passed and if not, why they failed.

A practical approach to this is:

The client writes scenarios. For example, in a shop-based system they may explain that a customer with a receipt can exchange items they have bought for at least the value of the item but no change is ever given. The returned item must be logged back into the stock pool.

You and your client have a meeting to clarify the details and make sure you have a mutual understanding of the scenario.

You write one or more acceptance tests for the scenario and check it with your client. This would include the specific data you plan to use for each test and, if updating files, the contents of the files you intend to change (you wouldn't want to change the wrong record would you!).

In large systems once acceptance tests have been agreed for a scenario, you involve other personnel from the company to develop more tests to explore all possibilities with an example to work from. For example, in the shop-based system above you might involve a range of shop managers from different branches to help construct tests.

Note the idea that your client understands their business and that you understand the technical ICT issues, and this technique allows us to merge the two together effectively.

After all the tests are completed, the client will either accept the system or identify changes which need to be made. When the changes are made and retested the acceptance test will also have to be repeated. It is highly unlikely that the user will accept that everything works fine just because you say that the change was made!

It is possible that your client may want the whole test performed again or perhaps just the problem areas to be retested.

 Coursework activity

Producing the documentation for your project

You can now produce all of the relevant documentation for your project. For example, a project that involves switching from one software package to another will certainly need a migration plan. You might well need training documentation, including an instructor's guide, a user guide and start-up or quick reference guide.

Changing software may have an impact on how jobs are done in your client's company and, if it is a large company, there may be procedure manuals to update showing new ways of completing jobs.

It is important that all relevant documentation is produced for your solution but only that which is appropriate. The documentation should be presented in a format suitable for your audience and should be professional or near professional in its appearance.

Last word

Commercial systems still fail and clients have to pay the price for this. All too often inadequate testing is a major factor.

Case study: Identity and Passport Service

In a rare, if unprecedented step, the Identity and Passport Service published the lessons learned from the failure of its EPA2 electronic passport application system in 2006.

Bernard Herdan, Executive Director, Service Delivery, Identity and Passport Service, explained why some online passport applications got stuck in the system leading to a backlog of some 5000 applications and the ultimate failure of the system.

'The user acceptance testing proved functionality and proved that all the various functions of the system worked OK but it did not prove the rate of throughput in volume. So once we started putting volumes of cases through, it [the system] worked fine to begin with but once the volume of cases began to build up then the performance began to degrade.'

Lessons learned from this meant the Identity and Passport Service increased the time allowed for acceptance testing from 9 to 18 weeks on its next project.

In this section you have covered:

- how to document the testing activities that you carry out
- how to approach the testing of your solution with users
- the types of documentation needed to describe a project
- which type of documentation would be needed for different situations.

15 Evaluating the solution

In this section you will cover:

- what is involved in providing a critical evaluation

- strengths and weaknesses in the context of an ICT solution

- how to evaluate your own performance

- how to structure a report for a given end user.

15.1 Evaluation

Critical evaluation

The quality of your completed solution depends heavily on whether your solution met the client's needs and was an effective solution to their problem or not. At the end of the analysis phase, you defined what would be delivered to solve the problem and the evaluation criteria that would be used to check the quality of your work.

Simply delivering the solution is not enough. If you intended to produce an absence monitoring system for a school that generated detailed absence reports each week you could create the system, but if it did not produce the reports with 100 per cent accuracy then it would be worthless. Equally, if the reports were not produced quickly enough for tutors to take action over missed lessons then your solution would again be worthless.

To complete a critical evaluation you must first of all have clear evaluation criteria. You will then need to assess honestly how well your system performs against those criteria, i.e. the criteria that you (and your client) set at the very beginning.

User/client report

Getting a report from your client is extremely valuable. Not only does it show that you have completed a real or realistic problem but it also provides you with plenty of material on which to base your own evaluation of how well you have met your client's needs. Ask your client to write the report on headed paper and sign it.

Your client should be commenting on the same criteria you set at the start of the project (which you could re-supply as a checklist) and the feedback they give can be very helpful to you in providing proof for any qualitative performance indicators, i.e. was the interface easy to use?

Your client should be critical and point out any problems or omissions. Your evaluation is more likely to be accepted as genuine if it has such criticisms included, than one that simply points out how good the project is in glowing terms!

Completing the evaluation

Assessment of success is achieved by specifying and measuring appropriate evaluation criteria that have accompanying performance indicators. Performance indicators can be quantitative, e.g. 'the system should be 100 per cent accurate' or qualitative, e.g. 'the user interface should be user friendly and intuitive to the user'.

Be honest in your evaluation work, as the ability to recognise faults in one's own system is an important skill. This will include any limitations found. For example:

To increase the processing speed of taking an order:

> In the existing system, it could take up to fifteen minutes to process an order. I would like to reduce that to a maximum of two minutes per order.

> This goal has been successfully achieved. Having timed the order creation process for a range of quantities and possible items I have found it would take an inexperienced user less than two minutes, on average, to order an item of stock, and after they have got used to the system, it is likely that they could do it in about one minute (evidence of this testing can be found on page 00 and user evaluation is on page 00).

Alternatively...

To increase the processing speed of taking an order:

> It could take up to 15 minutes to previously process an order. I would like to reduce that to a maximum of two minutes per order.

> This goal has not been achieved. Having timed the order creation process for a range of quantities and possible items I found it took an inexperienced user more than five minutes, on average, to order an item of stock. Comments made by the user during acceptance testing (page 00) show that unless the user knows the stock code they cannot enter the item correctly. I have found that the code is not always known, forcing the user to look it up in the paper catalogue and so while the facility works it cannot do so in the time specified.

This shows that even if your solution is not entirely successful you may still perform well in the evaluation section.

You must:

■ use evaluation criteria and performance indicators (where applicable)

■ refer to evidence for your statements, usually in the testing

■ and be honest!

If you have not tested the solution then it will be very hard to evaluate what you have done, as you will have no evidence to base your conclusions on.

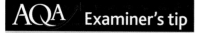 **Examiner's tip**

'Critically evaluate' means that you should include evaluation that identifies the strengths and weaknesses of the solution.

 Coursework activity

Evaluating your system

Now you should critically evaluate your solution against the evaluation criteria and your client's needs. You will be able to provide evidence from your testing.

■ 15.2 Improvements and enhancements

Your evaluation has allowed you to identify weaknesses and you should also be able to comment on any necessary improvements. For example, in the second evaluation sample above, as the user does not know the code, a sensible improvement would be to provide a way of looking up the code when the description or name of the item is known.

As for enhancements, the scope of your solution should have been very clear from the terms of reference given at the start. Enhancements are then additional functions, which could now be added.

A good example is an invoicing system, which records customer names and addresses, along with the products purchased. You could now extend this system into marketing, targeting customers with particular purchasing histories and using mail merge facilities. The software you selected to store the data is also compatible with your client's word-processing package, making marketing not just theoretically but practically possible if the client should decide to proceed with this enhancement in the future.

Coursework activity

Improvements and enhancements

Return to your own project and include any possible improvements that could be made to the solution.

15.3 Self evaluation

This course requires you to identify your strengths and weaknesses in the approach you took to the work. A common difficulty in this section is being specific about how you have changed during the project.

You may find it easier if you focus on your achievements during this project i.e. areas where you have progressed or had to change to gain success. There may even be additional steps you can take and so discuss how you aim to progress further with an area of achievement you were pleased with.

What should you be evaluating then? Here are some suggestions of areas that might apply to you:

Challenges

Parts of the project, which you found difficult, but improved your performance to complete those challenges successfully by the end of the project, such as, for example interviewing skills. Perhaps you lacked confidence and through practice became competent at taking one-to-one interviews and there will be evidence in the analysis section of your project to back this up.

Motivation

Did your motivation improve as the project continued? Did you achieve success, which inspired you to carry on? Alternatively, did you find it hard to maintain your levels of motivation throughout the project? If so, what did you do to ensure that you still met your objectives? What would you do in the future?

Learning styles

Maybe you have discovered ways in which you learn best from working through the project activities, for example, you enjoyed working as part of a team.

Tackling tasks

How did you go about the project? How was your time and task management? Did you keep to all the deadlines? How organised were you handling all the different resources? Did you have to change to deal with them better? What techniques would you use if you had to do a similar project in the future?

My interests

Have you simply come across things which you enjoyed doing and would like to know or learn more?

My courses

Perhaps you have discovered how different subjects can fit together, for example some aspects of human computer interface design need to consider psychological issues (short term versus long-term memory).

Importantly, as you focus on the ideas and issues relevant to you make sure that there is some evidence to back up your ideas and demonstrate that the strengths are indeed strengths and that your weaknesses have been addressed. If you lacked confidence in using HTML, but you were able to improve, you should have testing in your project to prove that the code you wrote now works successfully!

Once you have identified at least two distinct strengths and two weaknesses you are ready to write up your self-evaluation as the last part of your project.

 Coursework activity

Self evaluation

On a separate page identify an achievement, something you were pleased with, or proud of, in this project. You can then use the sheet to think about this achievement in more detail to evaluate your performance and so identify your strengths and your weaknesses.

■ What have you achieved? This means what has changed for you. Is there something you can do now that you could not do before? Is there something you now understand that before wasn't clear?

■ Importance? Why is this achievement important? What does it mean to you?

■ Evidence? How do you know what you've achieved? What specific evidence do you have? This should be something within your project, perhaps a skill you have acquired.

■ How did you get there? What specific actions did you take?

■ Next steps? Can you build on what you've achieved? Is there a next step? Are there still aspects you would like to improve that would make an impact on your performance in the future?

This final phase will help you establish if there are still areas for improvement that you could continue with.

■ Remember

Check the marking grid. If you haven't worked with this beside you throughout the project, check your work against it now. Make sure that you really have covered every criterion.

Good luck!

In this section you have covered:

■ how to complete a critical evaluation of your solution

■ how to describe improvements and enhancements in your project

■ how to complete a self-evaluation.

Index

Note: Key terms are in **bold**

A

acceptable use policy   39
acceptance testing   160–2
accounting systems   14
activities, information needs   5–6
adaptive maintenance   49
agile development
    methodologies   56–8
aims   130
alpha testing, testing and
    reliability   74
analysis, systems *see* investigating
    techniques; systems analysis
approval to proceed   45
attribute   65, 65–7

B

back office systems   17
backup and recovery
    large scale systems   80–6
    security policy   37
**BACS (Bankers Automated Clearing
    Service)   6**
beta testing, testing and reliability   74
bioinformatics, future
    developments   115
black box testing   48
brain-controlled computing, future
    developments   114
business case   129
business process   136
business process modelling tools
    data flow diagrams   64–5
    flowcharts   62–4
    information flow diagrams   62
    SSADM   62
    system flowcharts   62–4
    systems development tools/
        techniques   62–5
buying services   103

C

change control, security policy   37
change control, testing and
    reliability   73–4
Chief Information Officers   28
client needs, investigating
    techniques   133–5
collaborative working systems   20–1
common ICT systems   14–15
communication resources   108
Computer Misuse Act   41
consumables, internal resources   109
context-sensitive help   93
contract of employment   36
contracting services   104–5

Copyright, Designs and Patents
    Act   41
corporate strategies   32–4
corrective maintenance   49
critical evaluation
    evaluating the solution   163–4
    Examiner's tip   164
Critical Success Factors (CSF)   13
CRM *see* Customer Relationship
    Management
crystal, agile methodologies   57
CSF *see* **Critical Success Factors**
current system
    description, investigating
        techniques   136–40
    overview, investigating
        techniques   135–6
Customer Relationship Management
    (CRM)   23–4
customers, information needs   9–10

D

data analysis, investigating
    techniques   140
data decomposition diagram   46
data flow diagram   46
data flow diagrams, business process
    modelling tools   64–5
data mining   23
data modelling tools
    entity attribute diagrams   65
    entity relationship diagrams   65–6
    systems development tools/
        techniques   65–7
data portability   16
data protection
    legislation   10, 31, 32, 36–7, 40
    policies   36–7, 40–2
Data Protection Act   10, 31, 32,
    36–7, 40
data recovery point   80
data transfer, security policy   37
data transferability   16
data vs information, Examiner's
    tip   4
data warehouse   24
debugging   48
Decision Support Systems (DSS)   23
deliverables   45
design, system *see* system design
designing testing, testing and
    reliability   73–5
detail, Examiner's tip   17
development, ICT solution,
    Examiner's tip   79
development methodologies   55–8
    agile   56–8
    iterative   56
    linear   56

dialogue flow diagram   143, 143–4
disaster recovery strategy   80, 104–5
disciplinary procedures   36
document management
    systems   20–1
documentation   156–62, 158
    see also project report
    Examiner's tip   79
    installation   79
    types   156–8
DSDM *see* Dynamic Systems
    Development
DSS *see* **Decision Support Systems**
Dynamic Systems Development
    (DSDM), agile methodologies   58

E

e-commerce systems   24, 24–5
    security of data   25
e-room, systems   21–2
**EDI (Electronic Data
    Interchange)   6**
emerging technologies
    entertainment   112
    Examiner's tip   115
    future developments   110–13
    GPS technology   113
    mobile working   110–13
    RFID   113
    semacode   113
    ubiquitous computing   112–13
enhancements/improvements,
    evaluating the solution   164–5
enterprise systems   23
entertainment, emerging
    technologies   112
entity   65, 65–7
entity attribute diagrams, data
    modelling tools   65
entity relationship diagrams, data
    modelling tools   65–6
evaluating the solution   163–6
    critical evaluation   163–4
    improvements/enhancements   164–
    5
    self evaluation   165–6
evaluation criteria, investigating
    techniques   140–1
evidence, testing   159
examination-style questions   117–21
Examiner's tips
    critical evaluation   164
    data vs information   4
    detail   17
    development, ICT solution   79
    documentation   79
    emerging technologies   115
    feedback, client   150
    Health and Safety at Work Act   42

HWLC LEARNING CENTRE
EALING GREEN